Practical Grief: Stories of Loss and Love
Written by the Rev. Dr. Jules Erickson

Being a pastor is a duty and delight, hard work and a ton of laughter, heart stopping grief and joy.
This book is my attempt to pay tribute to many of the lives that have impacted the Ministry of Word and Sacrament as an ELCA Ordained Pastor.

Endorsements

"I have long felt an appreciation for the term ponder. It may be the simple pondering of what to have for dinner. It may be the beautiful words of Luke "Mary treasured up all these things and pondered them in her heart". With this book, Jules has provided us a gift of words to ponder. Words that are not steeped in academia, but based on real life experiences and purposeful personal insight."
Sheri Ramaker, R.N.

"I love surprises" those were the words he gave her. My husband died when our daughter was just three and that afternoon she awoke yelling that she'd seen her Daddy. I asked her if he looked happy and she said he did. She said "but he was so bright I couldn't look at him". I asked her if he said anything and she said "He said, "I love surprises." I knew then that he'd seen the other side and wanted me to know. As he was dying we spoke about what it might be like to die...he said he had doubts about there being anything at all and I would always say "I wish I could see your face when you get there...you're going to be so surprised." Jules was with me during those days...she walked beside me in my grief and despair. When I told her the story she made it the theme of his life celebration and turned that day into something that changed people's view of grief and death.

I was told by more than one person "I woke up that day so sad that I was going to bury my friend and I went home so full of hope and joy" I'll never forget what it felt like that day; to really celebrate a life, a person's journey here on earth and honor whatever happens when we've left this place and shed this body. Life is full of surprises but surprising others with the hope of everlasting life turns out to be the best by far.

I have found grief to be an intricate and unavoidable part of life. We grieve our loved ones. We grieve our lost dreams. We grieve our youth and the innocence of our children as they grow and sometimes stumble on the way to their own paths. I've come to understand that grief is not something to avoid. It is as necessary as air and even though sometimes it brings us to our knees, without it we would never grasp the true meaning of gratefulness.

Grief hurts and grief changes but grief is also a kind and compassionate teacher.

I have come to view the loss in my life as a part of my story, I don't try to hide it nor do let it define me. It is sacred to me so I honor it but I don't wear it on my sleeve. I dance with it in the quiet places in my life where the music never stops and then I step back into the day in awe.

- Sandi Alexander Whalen

Disclaimer: The words written in this book are meant to help navigate grief through meeting people where they are at. If you are "activated" by these stories, all used with permission, find a good Cognitive Behavioral Therapist.

These are my opinions and do not reflect the ELCA

No part of this book may be copied or reproduced without permission from the author.

Copyright © 2025 A Cracked Pot Studio™

Written by: The Rev. Dr. Jules Erickson
Cover Art: The Rev. Dr. Jules Erickson

Title Name: Practical Grief: Stories of Loss and Love
ISBN: 979-8-218-52467-8

To those who have
lost & loved,
this is Practical Grief.

CONTENTS:

Introduction		1
Chapter 1	Grief and the Family System	5
Chapter 2	Good Boundaries	29
Chapter 3	Don't Be An Asshole	45
Chapter 4	Suicide Sucks	55
Chapter 5	The Mobile	76
Chapter 6	Complicated Griefs to Bear	83
Chapter 7	The Queen Mum	101
Chapter 8	The Matriarch Died	107
Chapter 9	Tragic Grief: A Murder and a Death of Two	114
Chapter 10	20 Years Ordained: a Reflection on Betrayal	119
Chapter 11	Funerals vs Weddings	126
Chapter 12	Why Empathetic Preaching Is A Bad Idea	130
Chapter 13	A Grief Absorbed, Sort Of	145
Chapter 14	A Few Grief Examined and Examen-ed	151
Chapter 15	Sermons for Parent(s) Who Are Grieving	162
	If You Fall, I'll Fall With You	
	Holding On	
Author's note		173

An Introduction

In the Horizon Court onboard the Royal Princess, a repositioning cruise from Fort Lauderdale, Florida to Normandy, France, I sat opposite a Security Officer named Andrew. He was from Northern Ireland, served in the British Armed Forces and then as a police officer in Ireland for over twenty years before coming onboard as an officer on the seas.

I asked Andrew, "What is the most difficult part of your current position?" He said, without missing a beat, "Jumpers." I didn't ask him to elaborate; the look of sadness on his face said it all. Andrew then went on to tell me that his wife died just six months ago. "We were all there, she'd beat breast cancer ten years ago but when it returned it was swift. Our kids were there with us when she died."

He went on to talk about how the Protestant funeral and the events leading up to it happened so fast that it was over before he knew it. His wife's body had been cremated, the service conducted, inurnment: over. Andrew said, "Maybe the Roman Catholics have it right: big wake, drinks, memories, and a celebration of life." I said, "Maybe a less sanitized process?" He agreed.

We, in America, swiftly move from death to urn before any of our hands touch the cold flesh of our beloved ones. Both authors on death and dying, Kate Breastrup and Caleb Wilde discuss the disservice we do when we fail to allow family and friends to be a part of the death process – not just the dying process.

If you were born before 1960 you may remember homes having a parlor. In days gone by the body of the deceased would remain for a day or more until the friends and relatives could bid their farewells.

Our Jewish friends bury the body a day after death but then they sit shiva – a seven day period of time when they have no need for shoes because they don't leave the house. In fact, there is no music, no sex, and no dancing during that solemn timeframe.

I think we can learn quite a bit from other traditions. I also believe we, as a culture, a society, can be better at our own grief work by understanding more about the nature of grief from several perspectives: physical, emotional, and spiritual.

As an ordained pastor since 1996 in the ELCA I have been a witness to a wide variety of ways people respond to grief and loss. I have experienced my own deep grief in service to families who were devastated by death, over and over again.

After leading a class on Grief in the Family System over the last seventeen years at a local funeral home for their "After Care Program", I have learned a bit about grief that you may find helpful. This book is for people who have experienced loss, those who are preparing for loss, and those who simply want a few more tools in their kit as they navigate life.

I'm not sure where I heard it, but someone once said, "All counseling is grief counseling." I've thought about that for well over a decade and I believe it to be true. But in order for us to understand why that is true, I need to add that grief does not just concern death. It can be what some grief experts call 'ambiguous loss' which are things like divorce, a role change within a family, a move into a new community, a different job, or, the one that is often considered the most difficult to understand: the loss of dreams. The loss of dreams could be an altered future. It could be not walking your child down the aisle for a traditional wedding. The sky's the limit on loss of dreams, I'll leave ambiguous loss to authors and teachers like Pauline Boss and Ted Bowman.

This book is an attempt to put some handles on how we can understand grief from a different perspective, primarily by using Bowen / Friedman Family Systems Theory. These two men from the late 1960's through 1991 looked at the family as an entire system. You'll learn more about this in the chapter titled, 'Why Family Systems Theory Saved My Life.' In this book we will take a closer look at anxiety, the process of grief work (it is hard work!), myths, ridiculous platitudes, and how we can move through the dark, gloomy aspects of loss and toward a new adventure.

I'll conclude this work on a theological note from Dietrich Bonhoeffer and the rebel and brilliant author, Anne Lamott. Other nuggets that I hope may help you with Practical Grief will include: what to say, what not to say, and how to hold your sacred ground when others make assumptions about your own processing of grief – like one "prosperity pastor" recently wrote, "People should get over the loss of a loved one within 3-4 months." It's my opinion that pastors who preach "If you pray hard enough, God will give you a new car," are charlatans that often have a 'stained glass voice' that they turn on and off depending on their setting.

I'll also share with you some visual aids that may help all of us understand that grief is not a linear process. We don't go from A to B to C: done.

Finally, I'm going to tackle betrayal. Betrayal is one of the most difficult griefs to bear primarily because those affected by it are forced to let go of the fantasy or dream of what was imagined for the future.

Some of the poetry and songs might be repeated throughout this book. I tend to reuse certain pieces because they deeply resonate with me.

Whenever I preach, I am preaching to myself. I'm just glad people showed up. I mention this because when pastors are writing 'at' someone it falls into what I call 'bad practices'. The gift of being human is that we have a universal understanding of feeling big feelings and the little ones that pass along like clouds in the sky. When we take time to sit shiva with our losses, we can move through them with a pinch more of grace and self-compassion.

As an educator for KOK Funeral Home over the last two decades, one of the most valuable pieces people appreciate is their better understanding of Grief in the Family System.

The other tool I always offer up is the work by Kristen Neff. She offers meditations on the gifts of self-compassion. If you are experiencing deep loss, consider finding a therapist, pastor, priest, friend, imam, rabbi, or your family doctor. As I always say and believe, we don't go it alone, we were never meant to.

Chapter 1: Grief in the Family System

My education has had a profound impact on how I understand grief. I started my post-high school education at Concordia College in St. Paul, Minnesota. Back in 1986-87 it was steeped in the doctrine of the LCMS – Lutheran Church, Missouri Synod. My mother had been raised in this German Lutheran brand of faith down in Alpha, Minnesota. My father's parents went to two different churches, a Swedish (ALC) congregation and a Norwegian (LCA) congregation. The ELCA has gone through many mergers and transitions over the course of the last 50 years, which may be putting it mildly. Now, in 2018, my parents and my partner and I are active in the ELCA.

Since I left Concordia College, primarily because of some of their political and social justice stances, they have become a university that is quite diverse, open to new ideas, and, generally speaking, a place where education is of a high quality. Back in 1986-87 I had my first exposure to understanding the basic building blocks of grief education. The class was titled "Death and Dying."

What I remember from the class was two-fold. One, we do not talk about the dying process or death as a society. Two, the main book for the class was *On Death and Dying* by Elisabeth Kübler-Ross.

Again, I'll turn to Caleb Wilde for a spot-on explanation of my own experience in grief work.
A VERY POPULAR AMERICAN pastor recently wrote in one of his books that grief should only take a "few months." The pastor goes on to say something along these lines, *"You must get beyond it.*

Unless you let go of the old, God will not bring the new. It is natural to feel sorrow and to grieve, but you shouldn't still be grieving five or ten years later." As much as I disdain this passage of his writing, it's not entirely his idea, since so many of us believe the end of grief work should be closure. Where does this idea that we should "let it go" come from? Why do we, especially Americans, feel the need to "get beyond it" to find closure with our grief and our deaths?

I suppose many of us have the idea that we should find closure because we have a misinterpretation of Elisabeth Kübler-Ross's "Five Stages" model. It's important to know that Kübler-Ross never intended her model to be applied to grief – it was an observation of those going through the dying process. In her work with terminal patients she noticed that the dying would go through stages of denial, anger, bargaining, depression, and acceptance. (133).

The interpretation that many people have is that grieving is a linear process. But as Wilde wrote, the feelings surrounded those who were actively dying, not those who were left behind to grieve. Furthermore, the American pastor who suggested we need to 'get beyond it' is likely a person that has not experienced deep grief on a personal level.

Kübler-Ross was the main textbook. That was it when it came to books on grief, at least back in the late 1980's. I took leave of Concordia, found no direction while at Mankato State for one year, so I returned home to get my bearings and to sort out what I was 'called' to become. During that year off from a residential college I was a waitress, delivery driver, and cook at Carbone's Pizzeria in Eagan, Minnesota. When I wasn't working I attended Inver Hills

Community College. The classes that most intrigued me were Psychology 101, 102 and Adolescent Psychology.

When I entered into the seminary in 1991 I attended practicums and pastoral care and counseling with practical applications in institutions such as hospitals or care centers. Where I felt most at home was, and is, meeting people in their vulnerability and struggle.

On one of my first assignments I was sent to a transitional care center and nursing home on the border of St. Paul and Minneapolis. The year was 1992. The year is significant because AIDS was still widely and wildly misunderstood. Having been the director for my high school blood drive in 1986, I understood how HIV was transmitted. Even back then there were classmates who refused to give blood because they thought they would be infected with the virus.

People living with HIV / AIDS were often treated with disdain, fear, and hatred. To a certain extent, this is still true two decades later. As I walked the halls of the transitional care unit I had been assigned, I met a man who was dying from this brutal disease. The first time I met him he was relatively lucid. He shared stories about his life. He was funny and kind. The second time I saw him he had thrown up his lunch all over his face and dressing gown. The vomit was dry and crusty. No one had been in to clean him up, to treat him with any amount of dignity.

I did what was natural. I wet a cloth, wiped his face, and stayed with him until he fell asleep. As I worked on cleaning him up, staff hurled insults into the room like hate grenades. One phrase I remember was, "You fucking faggot. You got what you deserve." I'll spare this page any more injury. What did I learn? Compassion. No one deserves to be treated in such a dehumanizing way: no one.

Later on, while still in seminary, I served a concurrent Clinical Pastoral Education unit while serving a two-point parish in south-western Washington state. A two-point parish in this case was an old white clap-board parish on the top of the hill of LaCenter and a small satellite church held in Woodland, just off of Interstate 5, about five winding miles down the foothills of the Cascade Mountains. We were in the shadow of Mount St. Helens. If you looked directly south, one could see two-thirds of Mount Hood. It was a beautiful setting to live and work.

The clinical work took place in Portland, Oregon at Emanuel Hospital. This was about a thirty-minute drive on a good day from the parsonage at Highland Lutheran in LaCenter. My CPE supervisor was excellent. We had a good small group, too, which can either make or break the experience for interns in the CPE program.

Two of the books we were asked to read were by Alice Walker, I Know Why the Caged Bird Sings and The Color Purple. Between these two powerful works and the integrative teams I served on at Emanuel, I learned that the answers to most complicated ethical issues are rarely binary. As humans we like clear cut answers. We like to know what is right and what is wrong. We like answers like yes or no. That's binary. In recent days, non-binary is used to describe people who do not fit a gender or gender identity as clearly either male or female.

Because I was assigned to neonatal intensive care and adolescent intensive care, one of the topics we wrestled with was abortion. Even in recent years the issues surrounding abortion have caused great tension and division within the church. What I learned, after CPE and other training, is that abortion has to be taken one case at a time. Also, if people want to pick one side or the other, I will drop back into a position of learning and listening. There have been times when push has come to shove around this highly emotional and sensitive topic and I have been verbally attacked just because I represent clergy. When people have been adamant about me adopting their position, I direct them to the ELCA's statement on Abortion and back away.

All of that aside, part of the reason we have opinions in the first place is because we were raised with a particular family during a particular time in history. This is called our "Family of Origin." The Family of Origin is the family we grew up in.

This idea was further developed by the work of Murry Bowen, Edwin H. Friedman, and Michael Kerr. The focus of their research is called, "Family Systems Theory." It wasn't until seminary that I learned about this theory from a book by Friedman titled *From Generation to Generation*. To be totally honest, I did not understand most of what I read. I read it but I didn't get it. This was true for most of my higher education. I struggled with comprehension more than your average bear – to such a degree that I barely completed my Master of Divinity degree in 1995. Going to seminary is like no other higher learning institution.

Most of us enter seminary with hopes to preach the good news of Jesus' life, teaching, healing, death, and resurrection, only to have most of our hopes and dreams for a utopian future in parish ministry crushed. A colleague of mine once described seminary in this way. Imagine an old, traditional white clap-board church. It's pristine, beautiful. Maybe a little paint is peeling here and there, but it seems to have really good bones. Now, imagine a wrecking ball and bull-dozer tearing it down bit by bit. That is what happened to me during my seminary experience.

Everything I thought I knew about the Triune God – from my core beliefs to the doctrine of the Church – was destroyed. Toss in Church history, Koinë Greek, Hebrew, Systematic Theology, and all the rest of the classes and the result was my brain on fire. My brain did not have a snowball's chance in hell. Also, as it turns out: there is no hell. So, there's that. Now, some people still believe in hell. I get that, the bible is a difficult book to sort out. However, if we teach a theology of grace instead of a theology of fear, then I will err on the belief that many contemporaries live, teach, and preach: we have been given the abundant life now and forevermore because of Jesus' death and resurrection. The focus is on the resurrection. Always.

It wasn't until I went to Lutheran School of Theology at Chicago that I started to study Family Systems Theory. In fact, I recently wrote about the impact the theory had in my life in an article for Faith+Lead through Luther Seminary, St. Paul, MN.

Here it is in its entirety:

Bowen Family Systems Theory Saved My Life,
Jesus Saved My Soul

BFST is the abbreviation for Bowen Family Systems Theory and BSFT always reminds me of the word 'breakfast'.
(I love a good breakfast). [1]

I was having heightened anxiety as I navigated my way through a Doctorate of Ministry in Preaching at Lutheran School of Theology in Chicago. Well into my second call, I found myself getting 'activated' by one of the staff who would, in turn, talk to another staff person and my world would go upside down and backwards.

My advisor, Connie Kliengartner, now deceased, helped me learn about BFST through the lens of Rabbi Edwin Friedman, who wrote the book *A Failure of Nerve*. Currently this book is challenging because it was written a long time ago and Friedman does not share the same sort of political correctness that Luther Seminary and many other institutions subscribe to, which means, I'm not endorsing his book.

I will endorse BFST, *Friedman's Fables* (written by Ed Friedman), and an outstanding primer on BFST by R. Robert Creech, *Family Systems and Congregational Life: A Map for Ministry*.

---

[1] https://faithlead.org/blog/bowen-family-systems-theory-saved-my-life-jesus-saved-my-soul/

Why do I believe that BFST saved my life? Well, because I was starting to have anxiety attacks, I was getting caught up in wicked triangles, and I was not functioning well. I honestly thought that it was my responsibility to quell the anxiety within the system I served. As it turns out, the only way we can affect a system in a healthy way is to become more healthy ourselves.

What road did I take to get from stressed to the max to becoming a non-anxious presence? I read. A lot! I read authors specific to BFST: Roberta Gilbert, Israel Galindo, Peter Steinke, Murray Bowen, Michael Kerr, and the authors I mentioned above. I also started to practice what I was learning with other students of BFST. And, I attended seminars through the Lombard Peace Mennonite Center in BFST. I learned that I needed to go back to my Family of Origin and work things out so that I did not carry over unhealthy patterns to the parish I serve. This also enabled me to begin to notice patterns in all sorts of 'systems': church, schools, small and large government entities, and the like.

BFST has eight core concepts in its original form.
1. Triangles.
2. Differentiation of Self. Also known as Well Differentiation or Self Differentiation.
3. Nuclear Family Emotional Process.
4. Family Projection Process.
5. Multigenerational Family Transmission Process.
6. Emotional Cut-Off.
7. Sibling Positioning - adopted from Walter Toman.
8. Societal Emotional Process or Societal Regression.
9. Michael Kerr added two more: The Unidisease.

10. Supernatural Phenomena or Spirituality.

After leaning into BFST as a lifestyle, which as I stated above is also a 'practice', I started reading the work of Dr. Brené Brown, a Social Worker and Professor. She has incorporated many of the concepts of BFST into her work, podcasts, books, and Ted Talks. She makes BFST accessible to a much broader audience; she puts handles on a theory that can be daunting and hard to understand at first glance.

B.R.A.V.I.N.G.
Brené Brown is really, really popular right now. She is a researcher and a storyteller on the topics of vulnerability, being in relationships of trust, and what it means to belong. Her most recent book, *Atlas of the Heart: Mapping Meaningful Connection* is a manifesto on how we can use language to make healthy relationships. Read it. Then, start using your words.

Because once we start to learn about things like triangles, over-functioning and under functioning, togetherness force and individualization, we can be set free from our anxiety - at least to a more healthy extent.

Brené Brown discovered one of the best tools that I have absorbed into the essence of my being and my call as an ELCA pastor. The acronym B.R.A.V.I.N.G.

YES! We all want to be brave leaders, teachers, parents, partners, and all the rest, but HOW do we live being in 'right relationship' in a way that isn't dogmatic (black and white thinking)? How can we move our speech from "You make me so mad!" toward language that does not set up a 'shields up' response from someone? As in, "I feel really frustrated right now. Can we get curious about what just happened and come up with a way to navigate it in a healthier way for our relationship and the place we serve?"

Whoa! Did you see what just happened there? We moved from YOU language - often accusatory - to "I" language, setting a tone of wondering instead of attack.

The B.R.A.V.I.N.G. piece is from several of her latest books. I use it at the parish I serve as a 'buy in' for meetings, book clubs, and staff relationships. In fact, it has become so commonplace in our vocabulary around the church that people will pull me aside and say things like, "Pastor Jules, I need you to keep the vault on this..." My staff will say things like, "I need to set a clearer boundary with someone, can we talk about how to do that without hurting their feelings?" Also, when I am quick to make an assumption, I will ask myself, "Am I being nonjudgmental and generous right now?" (Usually, no. Bleh!)

Here is one of the best tools I have found to build trust and healthy systems as we lead, wherever we lead.

It's from her website, BrenéBrown.com:
"The acronym BRAVING breaks down trust into seven elements:

BOUNDARIES, RELIABILITY, ACCOUNTABILITY, VAULT, INTEGRITY, NON-JUDGMENT, AND GENEROSITY." For Brené's detailed definitions, go to: https://brenebrown.com/resources/the-braving-inventory/

Here's how I understand each of the elements as seen through BFST.

BOUNDARIES: This is the entry point for all of the elements of BRAVING to work well. I need to know where I end and someone else begins. In the theory, there is language around what is called a togetherness force. This is when we get sucked into other systems, both family and multi-family systems, and we find ourselves losing ourselves. There is a balance to be aware of in the theory. How do I not get globbed-together with that togetherness force and group think? How do I maintain my individual seLf as I abide (or paraklete[2]) with those I serve?
Here is where we have to know what we believe and what our core values are.

There's also another aspect to keeping good, healthy boundaries. We need to function well. All of us have a tendency to either over-function or under-function. The truth is, when we over-function, over work, and over think, we are actually under-functioning. The opposite of that is true, too.

When I have good boundaries, I function better and I am much more of a non-anxious presence. I also live my own motto: Clarity is next to godliness, not cleanliness - although I recommend both.

---

[2] PARAKLETE is one of the Koine Greek words for the Holy Spirit which literally means, the One who walks alongside of you.

RELIABILITY and ACCOUNTABILITY live in the same space for me. It's a simple phrase that I use to sum these two elements of BRAVING. "Say what you mean. Mean what you say. Follow through on what you said you were going to do."

VAULT: We keep other things confidential. This element is essential to shutting down triangles. Triangles are everywhere. We see them in situational comedies, dramas, novels, and everyday life. There is no such thing as a stable dyad. A dyad is two people. There is always a third entity in relationships. It may be two people and a job; two people and a dog or child. We need triangles to diffuse our anxiety. That is in the BFST. Where we get into trouble is when people pull us into their triangle. This happens all the time in church systems. As I mentioned above, when another person is talking about me instead of me, I get anxious.

The remedy for unhealthy triangles is to keep the vault, keep confidence, and redirect the person to discuss issues face to face with the person they are having issues with. Note: not by email, text, meme, or phone. Face to face allows us to pick up on the nuance of body language. It allows us to say: I see you, I hear you, and you matter.

INTEGRITY: Within BFST this is called being "Well Differentiated". As Christian Public Leaders we are called to be the beloved child of God that we already are and are becoming. This means that we are the same person at a church council meeting as we are on the tennis court. You get to be you. Everyone else is taken. We are not called to be shape-shifters, peace mongers, or willows in the wind, changing our opinion in order to make someone else happy. This takes courage. It is a practice and a lifestyle.

NON-JUDGMENT and GENEROSITY also live in the same camp for me. Maybe the person on the church council keeps bringing up scarcity within the stewardship campaign because they are dealing with their own financial history from the standpoint of the Multigenerational Family Transmission Process. Perhaps they came from poverty and cannot imagine ever having enough. Maybe they are doing the best they can be doing because of their past or their current situation. Using these two elements can not only help us stay out of judgment, they can also help us extend a generous spirit towards those who challenge us. Perhaps, challenging people are actually doing the very best that they can do in their present situation.

Non-judgment is also one of the more vulnerable parts of these elements because it is hard to ask for help. Sometimes it's hard to speak your truth and ask for what you need, yet, if we have courage to enter into hard conversations in a meaningful and respectful and curious way, our lives become less anxious. I know, I have practiced this element. Some days I get it right, some days, not so much.

Now, we did not get into the weeds with every BFST concept by using the BRAVING code for right-relationships. #6, Emotional Cut-off, for example, lives up to its name. I think it is important not to cut-off relationships, period, unless they are harmful or unlawful. I think about relationships in terms of a bridge. Some bridges can carry a great load and are built for semi's. Other relationships are tenuous and feel more like walking across a rope bridge on a windy day with a hundred foot drop.

The last piece of the theory that I have found incredibly helpful as a pastor is understanding Nuclear Family Emotional Process, Family Projection Process, and Multigenerational Family Transmission Process through using a Genogram. A Genogram is a family map that I draw when meeting with families as we prepare for a funeral. I also have couples preparing for marriage to draw each of their family genograms out and share their stories with one another.

As I mentioned before, BFST is a practice and a lifestyle. So is BRAVING. In fact, as a student of BFST for the last twenty years, I have come to see that each of the seven elements listed above fit well within the eight to ten concepts of BFST. (See Michael Kerr's latest book, *Bowen Theory's Secrets: Revealing the Hidden Life of Families*, for an expanded view on the added concepts 9 and 10).
BFST saved my life. I am continuing to work at being a Well Differentiated Leader, one who is non-anxious. When I started using BRAVING on a daily basis, my anxiety dropped, my work became more joyful, I became more playful, my relationships became more deeply loving and respectful, and, an added bonus, our parish became more healthy. Regarding both theories, there is one last piece of the puzzle that I'll leave you to consider: the more playful a system is, the healthier the system becomes.

I use BRAVING for staff reviews. I also use BRAVING for the times when I feel out of step with someone or they are out of step with me. It's a great tool and it makes BSFT much more accessible. I know BRAVING can help you, too!

< end of my article >

I had spent such a long time trying to be what I thought other people wanted me to be that when I actually started to implement Ed's interpretation of Bowen's Family Systems Theory, my head nearly exploded. Most true 'system's people' will tell you that it takes at least five years to understand systems and implement it into your own life. It is also true that most systems, whether it is a government or a church, will take the same amount of time to change. Systems theory moved me from emotionally reacting or interpreting people's feelings towards learning how to see the big picture.

The big picture is what Ed calls the 'stadium view.' Instead of getting caught up in the minutia of emotional anxiety, step back, gaaaaaayyyy back, and see what is going on from a less emotional perspective. In some ways this concept is similar to a study that focused on the time doctors spend with their patients. I looked all over for the actual case, but I have a feeling it was an interview on NPR over a year ago. The point of the study was that most doctors make a diagnosis within 15 seconds of listening to a patient's symptoms. If they listen even 15 to 30 seconds beyond the initial 15 seconds, the diagnosis changes nearly every time. We want the quick fix; our doctors want the quick fix. There is no such thing as a quick fix.

The only way I learned how to become well-differentiated was by practicing day in and day out. I learned to recognize my own pathology. I began to see how I was contributing to the anxiety. I started to see that anxiety is not a dragon to be slayed but rather an inanimate being; I learned how to quell my anxious reactivity towards highly anxious people by creating a different perspective. And, I started to understand how to use humor without donning the gear of a knight in armor – the sword of sarcasm wed with the heavy gear of steel venom. In fact, I began to realize that highly anxious systems are void of playfulness and humor; the opposite is true, too, if the system is more playful, the healthier the system.

In Edwin H. Friedman's book, *A Failure of Nerve*, I read words that transformed my ministry. "Stress and burnout are relational rather than quantitative, and are due primarily to getting caught in a responsible position for others and their problems." I began to understand that only I could be responsible for my own well-being. During the first ten years of being ordained, the relationships I had within the parish I was serving were not healthy. There were all sorts of weird triangles going on. A triangle is when one person does not speak directly to the person with whom they have a problem, but instead goes to a third party to hurl a complaint. Also, there was also the additional challenge of working with a peace-monger.

Ed says a peace-monger is a "highly anxious risk-avoider, someone who is more concerned with good feeling than with progress, someone who is so incapable of taking well-defined stands that his "disability" seems to be genetic, someone who functions as if she had been filleted of her backbone, someone who treats conflict or anxiety like mustard gas – one whiff, on goes the emotional gas mask, and he flits. Such leaders are often "nice," if not charming."[3]

---

[3] *A Failure of Nerve*, Edwin H. Friedman, page 13.

Yeah, I had a few of those roaming around my space. In fact, in some ways I was acting like a peace-monger because I was so afraid to be myself.

Again, this section of Ed's book made all the difference in why I think this theory saved my life:

I want to stress that by a well-differentiated leader I do not mean an autocrat who tells others what to do or orders them around, although any leader who defines himself or herself clearly may be perceived that way by those who are not taking responsibility for their own emotional being and destiny. Rather, I mean someone who has clarity about his or her own life goals, and, therefore, someone who is less likely to become lost in the anxious emotional processes swirling about. I mean someone who can be separate while still remaining connected, and therefore can maintain a modifying, non-anxious, and sometimes challenging presence. I mean someone who can manage his or her own reactivity to the automatic reactivity of others, and therefore be able to take stands at the risk of displeasing. It is not as though some leaders can do this and some cannot. No one does this easily, and most leaders, I have learned, can improve their capacity. (14)

Also, there is something to be said about salvation. I honestly thought that there was someone on the outside who could make my life better on the inside. I believed that someone would come and save me from whatever situation or person was challenging me. I was shocked to realize that the only person that could ever 'save' me was 'myself.' I don't know why that was, and to be quite honest, I usually blame the movie Jerry McGuire and the entire entertainment industry for selling such a stupid fairy tale. From the Princess Bride to just about every princess in Disneyland – someone is 'saving' someone else. Thank goodness Pixar and Disney started making movies in the early 2000's that actually show strong women and girls - none of whom need to be 'saved'.

Ed wrote, "The children who work through the natural difficulties of growing up with the least amount of difficulty are those whose parents made them least important to their own salvation." (201-203). My parents cannot save me, nor I them. We do not need to 'save' anyone except for ourselves. Furthermore, as a Lutheran Christian, salvation has already been given to us by grace through faith. There's nothing we can do to 'earn' it.

I had been trying to earn salvation on so many different levels that it was tearing me apart. I was angry and anxious, exhausted and burned out. I looked at articles and self-help books. I went to my primary doctor for advice. I saw a therapist. I wrote. But it wasn't until I read and started to intentionally put into practice this theory that I began to live my life with greater integrity. I also started meeting with like-minded system's people on a monthly basis to shore up my own leadership skills.

Since the system's theory saved my personal integrity, I have created much healthier relationships with my family of origin, my church family, and the greater ELCA. I have learned how to define myself and have grown a backbone – not to impress those around me – but rather to simply walk around upright. It has taken a ton of courage to get from where I was to where I am today. I have system's theory to thank for that reality.

Ed also wrote a whole bunch of fables to help people sort out their own family systems. One of my favorite stories is called "The Bridge." This fable is used with permission through the Bowen Trust.

This is the story of a man who had given much thought to what he wanted from life. After trying many things, succeeding at some and failing at others, he finally decided what he wanted.

One day the opportunity came for him to experience exactly the way of living that he had dreamed about. But the opportunity would be available only for a short time. It would not wait, and it would not come again.

Eager to take advantage of this open pathway, the man started on his journey. With each step, he moved faster and faster. Each time he thought about his goal, his heart beat quicker; and with each vision of what lay ahead, he found renewed vigor.

As he hurried along, he came to a bridge that crossed through the middle of a town. The bridge spanned high above a dangerous river.

After starting across the bridge, he noticed someone coming the opposite direction. The stranger seemed to be coming toward him to greet him. As the stranger grew closer, the man could discern that they didn't know each other, but yet they looked amazingly similar. They were even dressed alike. The only difference was that the stranger had a rope wrapped many times around his waist. If stretched out, the rope would reach a length of perhaps thirty feet.

The stranger began to unwrap the rope as he walked. Just as the two men were about to meet, the stranger said, "Pardon me, would you be so kind as to hold the end of the rope for me?" The man agreed without a thought, reached out, and took it.

"Thank you," said the stranger. He then added, "Two hands now, and remember, hold tight." At that point, the stranger jumped off the bridge.

The man on the bridge abruptly felt a strong pull from the now-extended rope. He automatically held tight and was almost dragged over the side of the bridge.

"What are you trying to do?" he shouted to the stranger below. "Just hold tight," said the stranger.

This is ridiculous, the man thought. He began trying to haul the other man in. Yet it was just beyond his strength to bring the other back to safety.

Again he yelled over the edge, "Why did you do this?"

"Remember," said the other, "if you let go, I will be lost."
"But I cannot pull you up," the man cried.

"I am your responsibility," said the other.

"I did not ask for it," the man said.

"If you let go, I am lost," repeated the stranger.
The man began to look around for help. No one was within sight.

He began to think about his predicament. Here he was eagerly pursuing a unique opportunity, and now he was being sidetracked for who knows how long.

Maybe I can tie the rope somewhere, he thought. He examined the bridge carefully, but there was no way to get rid of his new found burden.

So he again yelled over the edge, "What do you want?"

"Just your help," came the answer.

"How can I help? I cannot pull you in, and there is no place to tie the rope while I find someone else who could help you."

"Just keep hanging on," replied the dangling man. "That will be enough."

Fearing that his arms could not hold out much longer, he tied the rope around his waist. "Why did you do this?" he asked again. "Don't you see who you have done? What possible purpose could you have in mind?"

"Just remember," said the other, "my life is in your hands."

Now the man was perplexed. He reasoned within himself, If I let go, all my life I will know that I let this other man die. If I stay, I risk losing my momentum toward my own long-sought-after salvation. Either way this will haunt me forever.

As time went by, still no one came. The man became keenly aware that it was almost too late to resume his journey. If he didn't leave immediately, he wouldn't arrive in time.

Finally, he devised a plan. "Listen," he explained to the man hanging below, "I think I know how to save you." He mapped out the idea. The stranger could climb back up by wrapping the rope around him. Loop by loop, the rope would become shorter.

But the dangling man had no interest in the idea.

"I don't think I can hang on much longer," warned the man on the bridge.

"You must try," appealed the stranger. "If you fail, I die."

Suddenly a new idea struck the man on the bridge. It was different and even alien to his normal way of thinking. "I want you to listen carefully," he said, "because I mean what I am about to say."
The dangling man indicated that he was listening.

"I will not accept the position of choice for your life, only for my own; I hereby give back the position of choice for your own life to you."

"What do you mean?" the other asked, afraid.

"I mean, simply, it's up to you. You decide which way this ends. I will become the counterweight. You do the pulling and bring yourself up. I will even tug some from here."
He unwound the rope from around his waist and braced himself to be a counterweight. He was ready to help as soon as the dangling man began to act.

"You cannot mean what you say," the other shrieked. "You would not be so selfish. I am your responsibility. What could be so important that you would let someone die? Do not do this to me."

After a long pause, the man on the bridge uttered slowly, "I accept your choice." In voicing those words, he freed his hands and continued his journey over the bridge."

Some part of me had to die in order for something new to be born.

I had to let go of the rope. The rope of implied expectations. The rope of self-criticism. The rope of my own piety. The rope of shame. The rope that cut off my true personality from being celebrated by my friends and family. The rope of responsibility for another person's inability to function. The rope of allowing other people to define me.

Murray Bowen in his book, *Family Evaluation,* put it this way: "The courage to define self, who is as invested in the welfare of family as in self, who is neither angry or dogmatic, whose energy goes to challenging self rather than telling others what they should do, who can know and respect multiple opinions of others, who can modify self in response to the group, and who is not influenced by the multiple opinion of others." (By the way, 'Dogmatic' means having to be 'right' or to impose your opinion over and above everyone else's opinion.)

At some point, I realized that I had to become the person I was designed to be. I was reminded of that fact recently when a young person told me, "Pastor Jules, you just need to be who you are: everyone else is taken." This quip came up when I tried on a pair of goofy glasses without lenses that a 12-year-old was wearing. I crossed my eyes and made her laugh. Her mom asked her, "What do we say to people who think that we are weird or different?" She said, "Mom, you always say 'everyone else is taken – you have to just be yourself.'" Out of the mouths of babes.

Chapter 2: Good Boundaries

His name was Lowell, named after grandpa on the paternal side of the family. At just around a pound his skin was a translucent blue – the skin you could see beyond all the tubes and monitors strapped and taped onto his tiny torso. Lowell was a miracle. Jenny had been told that she'd never be able to have a child due to a cancer that compromised her womb. But there he was, there they were, in the alternative universe called the NICU (Neonatal Intensive Care Unit). Nick-U they call it – only those on the list can get in. I was on that list, mercy me.

The last time I'd been in this alternative universe was back when Ellen and Brian had Samuel. Sam was a smidge bigger than Lowell, but still 'undercooked' as NICU nurses say – those who do know the pain, isolation, and bizarre time continuum within the NICU.

As I write, Sam is now a strong wiry child with six-pack abs. He has a few challenges: like learning how to stop his perpetual motion, 'book' learning, and stopping his face from getting laugh lines by the time he's sixteen because it's stuck in a state of surprise and wonder. Joy and exuberance exhaust and delight his parents, and now, younger (bigger), solid 'little' brother, Daniel.

Sam's dad could slide his wedding ring over his wrist, all the way up to his shoulder – an image I'll never forget. Neither is the vision of Lowell: encased in a rectangular plastic cube with ports for hands to touch (not stroke) tiny hands and fingers. Babies this tiny can slough off skin instantly from even a tender touch.

I got the call on Thanksgiving Day 2008. The turkey was still in my stomach as I raced to the hospital that cold November day. As I entered the room, Lowell's mom and dad looked at me and said, 'it was time.' They decided they could not put off the baptism of their son any longer. A nurse came in with a sterile bottle of saline and a tiny plastic cup – the kind you use to knock back a shot of Nyquil when you just need the coughing to stop.

My throat was tight! My hands were unsteady. I placed them, triple washed, through the ports on the side of this new age cradle, cleared my throat, and said the words, "Lowell, child of God, you are baptized in the name of the Father, Son, and Holy Spirit. Amen."

There were hugs all around, tears in weary eyes – a call in the morning to tell me of Lowell's death.

We had a formal funeral in the church a few days later. Grandma rocked him beside his shoebox sized casket. When the family went to have their luncheon I stayed behind, with Lowell, because they did not want him to be alone in that big, blank space. We made our way to the cemetery and prayed our goodbyes as Dan, Lowell's dad, placed his baby boys' body in the ground.

A year went by and a new baby was born: healthy, vital, and well over five pounds. Now six years later they have five healthy, happy kids bouncing around their yard.

Every day is a learning experience, but some days are likened to 'come to Jesus and fall on your knees' in the ministry. During my internship I had been assigned to NICU and an adolescent ICU rotation for my Clinical Pastoral Care program in Portland, Oregon. I held crack babies, talked to homeless teenagers, and learned the value of medical ethics. It was all quite 'clinical.'

I thought I'd done a good job with Jenny and Dan as they walked the lonely road of Lowell's death. I followed up with them, attended his 'celebration of life' birthday party, and baptized each new child as they held them over the font. I thought all was well.

Then Dan came over to help me with some home renovations and said point blank: "I've been mad at you ever since Lowell died. I want you to know that I was really hurt because you did not cry; you seemed to show no emotion at all. How could you not feel our pain?"

I told him I had. Deeply. Privately. For weeks and even months.

He persisted, "Then why didn't you cry?"
I could have said, "It's not my job. You're not my family. I did what I was called to do."
Instead, I said, "If I started I might not have stopped."

The role of a pastor or chaplain or parent or grandparent is all the same when we baptize a baby who is not long for this world. We all break apart on the inside and try not to fall apart on the outside.

I cared. I still care. I loved all of them and felt only a sliver of their family's loss, yet I still had to keep it together through every hospital visit, the event of life and death and new life, and then death. Through the funeral and the placing of the shoe boxed sized rectangular box in a tiny dirt hole, I cared.

It was just too much.

I told all of that to Dan and he let go of his anger on the spot; another gift of grace. How do I know he let go of his anger? He had been leaning forward, red-faced, and raging toward me. Suddenly, after I said those words, "If I started I might not have stopped," he took a deep breath, sat back, and rubbed his face. It was a visual and physical transformation.

I was reminded of all of these emotions, this powerful learning experience, and the role of being a pastor when I heard a song, written and sung by Tony Norgaard, called "Paper Cup."

With his permission, I'll share the lyrics to his song:

Paper Cup
Close the door, we've got to do this right away.
Got to baptize all God's children before they slip away.

The nurses in the corner, softly start to cry,
to the lifeless body underneath the overhanging light.

And the chaplain cradled the child, lifted his head up.
Asked the nurse for water and he blessed a paper cup.

Back into your arms we give this child as you gave your only Son.
Pronounced him dead at 3a.m. when the baptism was done.

Close the door, we've got to do this right away.
Got to baptize all God's children before they slip away.

Mother holds her baby now, this child showered with love,
Love from here on earth, and a love from up above.

What a beautiful life – to know only love.

Here is the sermon I wrote for Lowell's funeral.
Lowell Thomas Vanelli – funeral sermon.

It was starting to snow this Thanksgiving when Jenny and Dan made their way to hospital.
Perhaps a little less than this bright white blanket today – but beautiful nonetheless.

I can only begin to imagine all the things that went through both of their minds as they drew nearer and nearer to downtown St. Paul.

It's not time.

No, really, it's not time – and along came Lowell Thomas Vanelli.

Long fingers, perfect little nails.

Long feet, ticklish when touched.

A beautiful, but too soon babe.

You both made the best of your time with Lowell; you got to know your son as best you could through wires and tubes.

Dan, your electrician's brain figured out most of the equipment that served your son, but I also heard that you were fixing down machines... making sense out of wires and cables – only a step away.

Jenny, you stood by Lowell's cradle, and watched with fascination as this little one moved his breathing tube around with tiny hands, seemingly to tell the doctors and the nurses what to do.

And, to be honest, when you said to me, "We are just so glad that we got to meet Lowell," tears jumped to my eyes – for they were some of the most beautiful words I'd ever heard in response to death.

I am amazed at your grace and dignity and poise over the last two weeks; for you have shown me what it means to be truly present in each other's lives and in your son's life.

Thank you.

Today, we mourn alongside you both.

We acknowledge that Lowell was a baptized Christian, a child of the water and the Word, a brother to us all.
Child of the same Heavenly Father.

We also pause to remember that Jesus gathers all of His children onto His lap.

In the stairwell just opposite of the fellowship hall where we will gather following this service, there is a painting of the gospel reading from Matthew. It shows Jesus sitting on a rock in a pasture surrounded by children, rosy-cheeked and smiling.

Parents were bringing their children to Jesus to have them bless them and pray with them.

Little Lowell was blessed, too, with prayers and touch and tenderness.

And I have no doubt that he is being swaddled on Jesus' lap this day.

At least that is what I hope we all hold fast to: that God will gather us all in and hold us close when we return to our first home.

I am reminded, too, of Psalm 139 which expresses how well God knows us – even when we're as little as Lowell.

"Oh yes, you shaped me first inside, then out; you formed me in my mother's womb.
I thank you, High God – you're breathtaking!

You know exactly how I was made, bit by bit, how I was sculpted from nothing into something.

Like an open book, you watched me grow from conception to birth; all the stages of my life were spread out before you.

The days of my life all prepared before I'd even lived one day."[4]

Lowell was knit together bit by bit – Jenny, who carried him; Dan who generated him.

And while we mourn his loss, we, like Jenny, may someday be able to say: "We are just so glad that we got to meet Lowell,"

And for this we can all say: Thanks be to God. Amen.

Pause. Deep breath.

Fast forward to 2022.

Lowell's mom died. Jenny, Jae to those close to her, had been on and off the prayer chain after their last son was born. Jae had cancer prior to the birth of Lowell; he was a miracle. After his death, three girls and two boys arrived. Surprise!

In June of 2022, I received a phone call from Jae's dad. He told me things were not going well with Jenny. I went to their house and abided with this lovely family for a time. The next day she died. The time with her and Dan are some of the most tender moments I have experienced in ministry. It was a very sacred time.

---

[4] Taken from The Message, Eugene H. Peterson

Dan wrote this next section; it was a reflection he had about a sermon that I had given at some point. And, to be honest, I do not remember preaching any of it. That being said, the Word goes out and it does not remain the same. Here's what Dan remembered and shared with me.

Matthew 5:13-15
[13] "You are the salt of the earth; but if salt has lost its taste, how can its saltiness be restored? It is no longer good for anything, but is thrown out and trampled under foot. [14] "You are the light of the world. A city built on a hill cannot be hidden.

Let us look at the qualities of salt.

Salt has at least three unique qualities.

1. A little salt sets the flavor in food.
The fellows with whom I eat breakfast from time to time are always amazed when I take a salt shaker and sprinkle a smidgen in a cup of coffee. "I've never seen that before, " they exclaim. Why do you do that?" I answer, "it takes the bitterness, and the bite out of the coffee."
Salt sets the flavor in food.

When we lived on the coast of NC we learned about "corning" seafood before cooking it. This is done by placing the food in a brine of salt. Allow it to sit for about 15 to 30 minutes, then rinse it off until it has lost its saltiness. Then cook it.
Shrimp soaked in salt has a sweet succulent flavor that is much better than the way most of us eat them. Salt draws out the old

dead blood, and unclean parts of the shrimp and leaves it clean. When it is rinsed and cooked the flavor is unbelievably different from Shrimp cooked otherwise.

2. Salt is a preservative. Our ancestors used salt to cure food to be used later. Country Ham, Corned Ham, Beef Jerky, and salted fish were staples of their diets.

3. Salt has healing properties. It kills most germs on contact. It burns when it hits a raw spot, but is very effective in cleansing a wound so it can heal. "Don't rub salt in my wounds", is a statement often heard when a person is hurt from good advice.

A good Christian exhibits the qualities of salt.
 a. We add a better flavor to the life around us.
 b. We preserve the good of God's creation.
 c. We bring healing to the hurting people in our community.

What is a salty person? Life always adds new meanings, and flavor to words. It has its extremes and what it accepts as a norm.
Put in modern language a salty person is one who makes a positive contribution to society. A good example is a Sunday School Teacher who feels the responsibility of conveying the Biblical message to his/her class by teaching lessons and by living life by example.

A good teacher knows each member of the class, works on motivating each one of them to be excited about being a Christian. Helps individuals find themselves in the class and the church. Visits them when they are sick, and remembers special days in their lives.

These teachers realize that to do a good job they need always to be learning new ways to hone their teaching abilities, and improving personal relations.

One salty leader can make a tremendous difference in a congregation.

Here's what we pulled together for Jae's Celebration of Life.

Jenny (JAE) Holst Vanelli - Outline for the Celebration of Life

Welcome / Announcements

The Chicks: Godspeed - sung by close friend Greg Bigwood
https://www.youtube.com/watch?v=zOwxRpItEt4

Kids Message
Song: You Are the Light of the World, Dakota Road
https://www.youtube.com/watch?v=-eR8APAT0s4

Tributes:
    Marin and Dan
    Jill
    Bobbie, Janel, Kari

Song: If I could Make a Living out of loving you (lyrics projected)
https://www.youtube.com/watch?v=0q8-CwJYvfA

Scripture: 2 Cor. 5: 1-8, The Message version

5 ¹⁻⁵ "For instance, we know that when these bodies of ours are taken down like tents and folded away, they will be replaced by resurrection bodies in heaven—God-made, not handmade—and we'll never have to relocate our "tents" again. Sometimes we can hardly wait to move—and so we cry out in frustration. Compared to what's coming, living conditions around here seem like a stopover in an unfurnished shack, and we're tired of it! We've been given a glimpse of the real thing, our true home, our resurrection bodies! The Spirit of God whets our appetite by giving us a taste of what's ahead. He puts a little of heaven in our hearts so that we'll never settle for less.

⁶⁻⁸ That's why we live with such good cheer. You won't see us drooping our heads or dragging our feet! Cramped conditions here don't get us down. They only remind us of the spacious living conditions ahead. It's what we trust in but don't yet see that keeps us going. Do you suppose a few ruts in the road or rocks in the path are going to stop us? When the time comes, we'll be plenty ready to exchange exile for homecoming."

Homily: PJ

Jenny and Dan Vannelli and brought six amazing children into the world: Lowell, whom she is holding again, Marin, Leo, Maisa, Myla, and Lars.

I do not feel like I need to add a tribute after all of the amazing words of support that we have heard and read today.

What I'd like to do is remind you all that Jenny loved so well because she was so incredibly loved.

She created the feeling of a safe and welcoming home wherever she went. That is a pure gift, to feel seen, to offer a safe place to land, and to be at home in her own body which is now set aside like a worn out tent, a tabernacle, a holy place - especially now that she has returned to her first home.

I can only imagine what it was like to enter into that light and love.

That being said, she carried her light in such a way that left all of us with a feeling of gratitude - simply because we knew her.

To her parents, brothers, aunties, extended family, and her amazing group of friends, as well as her immediate family - I want you to hear how amazed I am at your care for her throughout her times of struggle.

Dan, you are an amazing husband. You know how to abide and you did so with grace and deep and abiding love. As you manage this thing called GRIEF, know that you are not alone. Let us know how we can help.

I'm reminded of a portion of Romans 8, from the same Message translation, that I thought Jenny, Jae, Jaebird might appreciate - notice the present tense - the veneer between this life and the next is thin in places. Right, Lowell?

Back to the words to the people of Rome.

"This resurrection life you received from God is not a timid, grave-tending life. It's adventurously expectant, greeting God with a childlike "What's next, Papa?" God's Spirit touches our spirits and confirms who we really are.
We know who he is, and we know who we are: Creator and children. And we know we are going to get what's coming to us—an unbelievable inheritance!
We go through exactly what Christ goes through. If we go through the hard times with him, then we're certainly going to go through the good times with him!"
The day before Jenny died she told me, "I'm not going to die; I am being made new from the inside out. I am not afraid."

I wonder if the Christ light she and all of us carry within us helped her with birthing from this life to the next?
I believe it did. And, now we all get to share our light with those who struggle with darkness and difficult times.
Today is a celebration of life, for Jenny and for all of us who shelter each other's lights and bring more light into the world one person at a time.

A Jewish parable reads, "Save one life; save the world."
Also, this.
I've used this reading at more than one occasion such as today from Jean Formo because I believe it is true.

Homecoming Party — Jean Formo (©1982)[5]

Death is God carrying us
in one arm while the other
flings aside heaven's door
to welcome us
back to the blazing hearth
of our first home.
while those inside,
having arrived before us,
rush to the door
like glad children shouting,
"They're here!" "They're here!"
Death has a bad name
on earth, but in heaven,
it's a homecoming party
every-time the door opens.
God does not forget
those earthbound children,
sad and left behind.

God leaves the party early
to enter into their despair and
to get them ready for their
own parties someday.

---

[5] Used with permission.

While we are having a party today, we can only imagine the homecoming party that is happening as we pray our "see you soon" prayers.
And for this good news we can all say: Thanks be to God! Amen.

Special Music HOME by Philip Phillips
Lord's Prayer
Commendation
10,000 Reasons (Bless the Lord)
Blessing

It is such a privilege to paraklete with so many good people.

The next chapter, well, Bill Whalen was a bit of a handful.

Chapter 3: Don't Be An Asshole

It was October 17, 2015 about 1:30 p.m. I had just conducted a funeral for another of a 'handful' of a man known as George Anderson. George was one of those guys who always had a joke for everyone, a joke that was never very good, I might add. This was not a difficult service to officiate: George was loved, he loved well, he had time to say goodbye, and, because of the nature of his illness, nearly everyone, and I'm guessing George would be included in this, too, felt relief that he was no longer suffering. It was a good death.

I was reminded of the Jean Formo quote from a poem she wrote to a dying friend, The Homecoming. You can read it again in the previous chapter.

Back to the day of George's funeral. You know you are late to a funeral when the pastor is leaving the building following the burial and luncheon. Enter Bill Whalen.

I walked to my car when a beat up old Aztec pulled into the staff parking and filled up two spaces at a 45-degree angle. Bill jumped out of the car, looked at me, and said, "Good! I missed the funeral." I said, "You're such an asshole!" He laughed and went inside, tipping his cap at me as he went. Fast forward about nine months. Bill Whalen is actively dying. I stop by his home, touched base with his wife, Sandi and their daughter, Adele, and mention this story to her, adding, "Maybe the last words I say to Bill shouldn't be 'You're such an asshole.'" Sandi nodded and Bill agreed to see me.

I'll include my portion of the service we created for Bill in just a couple of paragraphs that will explain more about how non-traditional funerals can open hearts to heal in ways that traditional funerals cannot. What I do want to mention here is that the conversation I had with Bill Whalen was profound, humbling, and brutally honest. It was sacred.

"Sacred" as described by Caleb Wilde in his book, *Confessions of a Funeral Director,* "is a word we need to reclaim. It has lost its meaning because we associate the word with religious connotations – something is only sacred if it has been sanctified by religion. It's definition that works in some cases, but beyond the religious connection, sacredness is defined by love. When something or someone is loved, that love sanctifies it. Our children are sacred. Our loved ones are sacred. And our aging and disabled loved ones are sacred because they are loved. Even our dead are sacred because though the body no longer works, it is still sanctified by the love of family and friends." (Pages 72-73).

What I will say about my sacred exchange is that I have kept the promise I made with him.

Also, one other thing: I love surprises!
"Bill Whalen's Service
You do not have to be good. You do not have to walk on your knees
For a hundred miles through the desert, repenting.
You only have to let the soft animal of your body love what it loves.
Tell me about your despair, yours, and I will tell you mine.
Meanwhile the world goes on.

Meanwhile the sun and the clear pebbles of the rain are moving
across the landscapes, over the prairies and the deep trees,
the mountains and the rivers.
Meanwhile the wild geese,
high in the clean blue air,
are heading home again.
Whoever you are, no matter how lonely,
the world offers itself to your imagination, calls to you like the wild geese,
harsh and exciting -- over and over announcing your place in the family of things.
- Mary Oliver, Wild Geese

Today we are going to remember Bill in a way he really would have liked: a party at a golf course with a mind-blowing view of the magnificent Mississippi River and drinks for everyone.

To Bill: Cheers.

We are going to speak some words, we will find time to laugh, to remember, and also to record this time together so that when Adele gets older she'll have more memories and reminders of her papa.

The video camera will be set up, following the service, for you all to share a memory, how you knew Bill, or a message for Adele and Sandi. Sign up for a time. Put your drinks down for the recording and lean in with a big smile.

My experience with Bill was limited; the formality of worship and church was not his cup of tea, but his desire to help people was more in line with Christ than Bill would lead us to believe.

You all know what I mean when I say that as a fact.

So being at a golf course and not in the confines of the building of a church I thought I'd share with you an exchange we had about a year into his cancer diagnosis.

Bill was running late for a funeral – really late – as in, I was leaving the building to go home. Just as he rolled into the staff parking area, I was rolling out to my car.

He tipped his hat to the side and said sarcastically to me:
> Oh, Good! I missed the church service.

To which I replied: You're such an asshole. (Insert laughter here). Welcome to Pastoral Care 101 class folks...

One week before Bill died I was out at the house when I mentioned to Sandi that maybe the last words I say to Bill are the not the ones aforementioned.

He agreed to see me.

I told him that I wanted to end on a higher note than our last encounter and recalled to him a cartoon that I keep wanting to put into the newsletter by David Walker, who hosts the website: The Naked Pastor.

It's a two-panel cartoon where a guy is walking with Jesus.
The guy says: What am I supposed to do again?
Jesus replies: Don't be an asshole.

You can only imagine the amount of delight Bill had in those beautiful blue eyes after that exchange.

My short time with Bill was one of the most profound moments in 20 years of ministry.
It came as not only a blessing but also a surprise.

Here's what I know to be true about Bill Whalen:

He was full of surprises: of grace and gratitude – for all you sticks in a bundle.
He liked to share his gifts.
He liked helping other people.
He loved his kids and nieces and parents and sisters.
He wanted to see everything in his travels: it was in those adventures he was fully alive in his own skin, happy.

Yes, Bill's life was full of surprises, starting at the very beginning of his life.

Surprise, born premature at just 4 lbs to a mother who was unable to raise him...

Surprise! - Argene stepped in, fell in love with him and raised him as her own.

He was raised with sister MJ but also, after learning of his biological mothers death,

Surprise - he had another half-sister who lived in Tucson.

DeeAnn and MJ turned out to be such a lovely part of his life, especially these last years.

Surprise, school uniforms, freckles, and coke bottle glasses made him uncomfortable but the friends he made along the way ended up being the coolest bunch of friends and stayed loyal to him till the day he died.

Surprise, after years of friendship and supporting each other through failed relationships, he and Sandi were married in 1995 and actually kept the promise, "till death do us part".

Surprise, I took a vacation to Costa Rica in 2000.

Surprise, they left with a Villa on the Pacific Ocean.
Next to Adele and Sandi, that place was what he called: the best gift ever.

Surprise, Adele, born to Sandi at age 47 – miracle baby, a child who looks like an angel and can still hear them, too.

Surprise, terminal cancer diagnosis just 3 and a half years to watch her grow and learn, time to say the things that needed to be said, beautiful, messy, blessed days.

Surprise: all the people who showed up, cleaned up, shopped, laughed, fixed stuff, installed fairy gardens and performed random acts of kindness – Bill asked me to say to all of you: Thank you.

Your love and support was nearly too overwhelming for words, for him, for Sandi, for Alex and Adele.

Sandi, I do have some surprise words for you.

Your spirit, your earth-mother, patchouli scented, glorious presence was an incredible gift to witness as you bore the weight of having 'death' move in.

It takes a very strong person to accept the help of others, to let them in your physical space, your vault of confidence, your vulnerability, and into your heart.

You have done all of this while being a care-taker, a mom, a daughter, a sister, and friend.

You not only deserve a pat on the back, you deserve a gold medal.

Grief-work is the hardest work we will ever do in this life – you've done that hard work and will continue to make your way through grief through the rest of your life.
But hear this if you hear nothing else today: well done.

You are amazing. (Applause started here).

One last surprise comment from me to Bill:

Go in peace, bud.

It was a joy to know you and to love you.

I promise, along with all of these people here, along with the ones who couldn't make it today: We will "keep watch over them" as I know you will do, too. Amen.

To Bill and to all of you I'll give you parting words from Sam Baker:

Go in Peace
Go in kindness
Go in love
Go in faith
Leave the day
The day behind us
Day is done
Go in grace
Let us go
Into the dark
Not afraid
Not alone
Let us hope
By some good pleasure
Safely to
Arrive at home
Let us hope
By some good pleasure
Safely to
Arrive at home

Bill has safely arrived at home. And for this good news we can all say: Thanks be to God."

That was my 'tribute' to Bill Whalen. It is true that death has a bad name on earth, but I also have seen a fair amount of good deaths, too. We have sanitized death. We can also create opportunities for families to lean into the dying process and the actual death by doing two things: talking about the inevitable (death) and showing up.

Sandi followed up this tribute with these words:

His two best friends and his wife followed with stories, memories, words of hope, grace and gratitude. There were tears, yes, plenty...but there was also laughter, much laughter, even big, buckled over, belly laughter. Perhaps it was the lovely location, the view of the river, eagles soaring by. Perhaps it was the greeters at the door handing out drink tickets saying, "Welcome! Have one on Bill." Perhaps it was the images in the slide show that included the end days as well as healthier times. Maybe it was the music the band played which filled the dance floor with spinning children, swaying old folks and everyone in between. Maybe it was the video interviews which offered an opportunity to have a part in the future healing of a little girl who will grow up without her Daddy. Maybe it was just the fact that the word "Asshole" was used multiple times somehow leveling everyone to an even playing field, uniting us in our "sinfulness", our "humanness". Whatever it was, the combination of all of it, no one could deny it was a real celebration of life that day and proof that "all of life is to be celebrated; even its ending". People still bring up that day and remark how special it was. One woman said this lovely thing... "If you had told me that morning that I was going to end that day with joy in my heart I would have never believed you. I was going to a funeral for a friend. I was sad, very sad. But when I laid my head down that night I felt joy and gratefulness. I felt renewed and refreshed. I was changed by that day."

Sometimes a pastor actually gets to see and hear the results of practical ministry. I'm ever so grateful for the warmth, love, and gratitude this family showed each other, all those who were able to gather to pray some goodbyes, and to me. I am honored and blessed to have known Bill Whalen.

Chapter 4: Suicide Sucks

Laura King had been toggling back and forth between two ELCA congregations in Cottage Grove for over a year when she died. I don't know what she was looking for, my guess is that she was looking for peace, deep and abiding peace. The sort of peace that is really hard to find when one is struggling with deep depression. Depression, as described by a colleague of mine, is like walking around with a wet, wool blanket draped over your head. You can see where your feet are taking you, but you have no idea where you are or where you'll end up. Simply stated: it is exhausting.

Laura's son, Phil, just 15 at the time of her death, came into my office in an embodied grief (shock). He said, "My mom just died and we're here to plan the funeral." So, we sat down, the family and I, and planned her funeral. A side note, I had no idea that she had died or that we were doing a funeral. A few hours later I found out that the other pastor at the other parish she had also attended had been waiting for the family to arrive. After I discovered this I called and apologized to the pastor who had waited for the family to show up. Who knew? The parish I serve did provide the funeral for this beloved saint.

When there is a suicide there is even more emotion within the family system. Some families want to share everything, others want to semi-cloak the details behind the death, still others end up in what I call the 'cone of silence.' Oftentimes that 'cone of silence' is steeped in shame and guilt. Shame, as in, I am a bad person because I believe I could have prevented this death – by my own two hands! Guilt follows right on shame's heels with ridiculous phrases like, "I wish I could, would have done x, y, or z." Or, the 'ought's' kick in. Also, the 'if's'... "If only I had _____."

When someone makes the decision to take their own life there is rarely any chance of changing their mind. At that point in time their mind is not functioning 'normally'. That's the terrifying reality of depression. It's filled with conspiracies and confabulations. Conspiracies are 'with' 'spirit' of a whisper of things that are not true.

Confabulations are 'with' 'story', as in, the story I heard or believed I heard has now become true and I will not or cannot change my mind about this new 'truth'.

I can remember my first experience with a suicide. My cousin, just nine months younger than me, took his life at age 15. I hardly knew Scotty. I remember him when we were little, mostly through photos and my parents sharing stories of how we were 'two peas in a pod' whenever we got together. Scotty's death left a deep wound on my own adolescent heart. I felt deep grief. And, what compounded it for our family was that we did not have a funeral; there was no closure.

We live in a culture that gets continually caught up in the question: Why? The 'Why' question can end up throwing us into what mental health professionals call 'perseveration.' Perseveration is a medical term that can be best described as the mind spinning in unanswerable questions or thoughts. Just imagine a gerbil on an exercise wheel in its abode. Squeak, squeak, spin...on and on and on, going: no where. Squeaking along, we find ourselves unable to get off the negative feed loop of the narrative we are caught up in, namely the 'Why's?' We long for the answers around that triad of phrases, like: I should have, I ought to have, or, if – I – had – only done x, y, or z.

Thoughts like those spin and spin because our minds long for closure. We want answers. Or, as Friedman in A Failure of Nerve: Leadership in the Age of the Quick Fix, suggests, we want a quick fix. Why did they die? I should have been able to help, right? That brings us back to the chatter in our heads.

Oftentimes when I meet with families, either before, during the dying process, or, after death, I will invite them to let go of the 'Why?' question. I'll suggest they take a vacation from the loss. It's too big to tackle when we're in full-blown grief. Nothing makes sense. Nothing.

I'm not suggesting that the question should never come up, that is part of being human. Yet, at some point humanity needs to recognize that death is a part of life. I am reminded of a quote by one of my favorite preachers and teachers of all time, Pastor Barbara Brown Taylor. She wrote, in her book *Home By Another Way*, "New life starts in the dark. Whether it is a seed in the ground, a baby in the womb, or Jesus in the tomb, it starts in the dark."

Back to Laura. She had been battling depression for years. She was tired. She was not in a place where she could make good decisions. That is the nature of depression.

Her family chose to share her struggle with depression – not the details of her death. Her children and husband, sister and her husband, and other family and friends gathered around her body before it went to be cremated. They were instructed by the funeral home staff to refrain from holding on to the body. They could touch her, carefully. She had not been embalmed. They cried their goodbyes, had time to get in touch with the finality of death, and then they released her entire being: body, mind, and spirit.

Her youngest asked that we play a song at the funeral home that may seem to most traditionalists to be unconventional. I am a pastor who believes that people need to be met wherever they are at. We played the song.

Was it a hymn? No. Honestly, I could have cared less. (Although, I do have a standing policy that weddings in the church cannot have Disney music, but that's a different book).

The song Alex picked was by the band Evanescence, song title "My Immortal."

https://www.youtube.com/watch?v=5anLPw0Efmo

These lyrics spoke to Alex and to her family. They served as a balm for healing. If a song can help the process of healing, perhaps the mainline churches, like the ELCA, could also consider more flexibility within funeral services instead of staying on the script that is given to us in our hymnals.

Which brings me to another suicide that truly sucked.

Sincerely, this was incredibly heart wrenching for every person who was affected by this unbelievable death. Josh was only 27 when he went up to his bedroom, loaded a shotgun, and killed himself. He and his wife had been married for just a few months. It was his birthday. It was also the early morning of Easter Sunday.

On Easter Sunday, just after the second service, I remember seeing his aunt taking a phone call. She was standing in the parking lot, dumbstruck. She came back into the church in a total panic. She told me what she knew, that Josh had died. That's all she knew.

What compounded the grief for this family was that they had celebrated their wedding on a beautiful Cancun beach at sunset. The state-side reception was scheduled for the Saturday after Easter. We held the funeral on Friday night, a day before the same people would have gathered, shared gifts, and toasted the young couple.

Joshua C. Koehler 27 of Rosemount formerly of Cottage Grove Died accidentally March 27, 2016. Josh was born March 26, 1989 to Karen & Noe in St. Paul, Minnesota. He grew up in Cottage Grove attending Park High School, graduating in 2007. He married his high school sweetheart Samantha Theno in Cancun, Mexico on January 22, 2016. Josh loved to spend time outdoors, especially hunting & fishing. He loved everything nature had to offer. His contagious smile and laugh will never be forgotten. He will be deeply missed by his loving wife Sammy; mom Karen (Duane) Jacobson, his dad Noe; siblings Dustin (Louise), Ashley, nephew Mason; nieces Mona, Mya; grandparents Bonnie & Ole Teigen; parents –in- law Ann (Bob) Theno; brother- in- law Tyler Theno; many other relatives and friends; furry companion Milly. Preceded in death by grandparents Jose & Maria; uncle Che Che. Memorial service 7pm Friday, April 1, 2016 at All Saints Lutheran Church (8100 Belden Blvd. Cottage Grove) with a visitation starting at 4pm.

When I sat down with the family to sort out the service I rolled out what we usually do in the Evangelical Lutheran Worship book: an invocation, prayer, psalm, and so on. With a guttural sob his wife, Sammy, said, "I don't want to do any of it!"

I asked, "Do you mean a funeral?" She said, "No, I know we have to do something, but not that." After more conversations, questions, and wonderings, we came up with a service that was fitting for this young man.

Was it unconventional? Yes. Did it fit Josh? You bet. Four of five of his closest friends shared stories that were funny, warm, and kind. The family wanted me to speak the truth around what happened without disclosing the details.
Also, they wanted me to address mental illness and how to go about getting help – especially in the wake of Josh's death.

Josh Koehler Service at ASLC, April 1, 2016
Show: Video of the Cancun wedding of Sammy and Josh. Brené Brown said in her book *Rising Strong*: "Yes, I agree with Tennyson, who wrote, " 'Tis better to have loved and lost than never to have loved at all." But heartbreak knocks the wind out of you, and the feelings of loss and longing can make getting out of bed a monumental task. Learning to trust and lean in to love again can feel impossible."

When we love someone, our hearts break open – that's how the light gets in.

Josh cracked open hundreds of hearts, it's why we gather here today in this place, to honor him as a husband, brother, son, cousin, grandson, friend, and child of God.
In the Lutheran church we have a service that is pretty formal.

It would not ring true to have something like that for Josh. We will not do that tonight.
What we will do is sing a song or two, remember Josh with affection, grace, and warmth; we will honor and celebrate his life and we will pray.

Sounds good?

Now, even though this song is out of our hymnal, Josh, as you all know, was a huge fan of being outside, being close to nature, and being a part of this incredible creation that we've been given.

Let's sing: On Eagle's Wings. This is a song based on scripture with the image of God lifting us up, especially when we are feeling very low. Look at the screen or turn in your hymnal to 787 and let's sing it together.

Readings.
The readings today have been taken from a variety of resources; they were chosen by Sammy and Josh's family and reflect some of the things he loved.

A Time for Remembrances – there will be a few folks who will read / talk on behalf of the family.

Can you imagine Josh dancing?

Do you have the image in your head?
Pretty much one move with a leg kick and a finger pointing.

Now, he loved this one song and he'd play it over and over again, particularly when he took a shower.
Dancing in the Moonlight – we'll have the lyrics up on the screen. If you know it: sing it. If you do not know it, read the lyrics. If you need to dance: dance. I think Josh would get a 'kick' out of that.

Homily

As much as you can: be here now. Stay with me for just a few minutes as we hear a little more about Josh. Today is April Fool's Day. It's a day where we play jokes and tricks on each other and have a good laugh. Josh's death screams for the line: April Fool's or Just Joking. None of us wants to be here tonight.

Here's what I know: April Fool's Day is a response to Easter. Here at All Saints we have had a Holy Humor Sunday the week following Easter.

We do this because the origin of April Fool's Day is that the "Joke" is on death.

Christians believe that because Jesus died and rose from the dead, death no longer has any power.

Yes. Death is a part of being human. And, grief is one of the hardest things we'll ever do in our lives.

Back to Brené Brown: "MANIFESTO OF THE BRAVE AND BROKENHEARTED:
There is no greater threat to the critics and cynics and fear-mongers than those of us who are willing to fall because we have learned how to rise with skinned knees and bruised hearts; We choose to own our stories of struggle, Over hiding, over hustling, over pretending. When we deny our stories, they define us. When we run from struggle, we are never free.
So, we turn toward truth and look it in the eye. We will not be characters in our stories. Not villains, not victims, not even heroes. We are the authors of our lives. We write our own daring endings. We craft love from heartbreak, Compassion from shame, Grace from disappointment, Courage from failure. Showing up is our power. Story is our way home. Truth is our song. We are the brave and brokenhearted. We are rising strong." [6]

You can all rise strong. That is the promise we are reminded of tonight. We are not alone in our pain and our grief.
God is with us through the people around us; reminding us again and again that we are worthwhile, capable, acceptable, and loved for free.

---

[6] https://brenebrown.com/art/manifesto-of-the-brave-and-brokenhearted/

God is with us as we wonder about the 'why' questions of life, of death, of daily living. In fact, I'd like to invite you to consider giving up the 'why' question.

Things happen. Josh was not Josh when this happened.
Try to let go of the 'why' and take stock of what's going on inside of you. (pause)...

Love deeply. Pay attention. Celebrate Josh's life, laugh, and wildly entertaining dancing in your mind's eye.

This life we have been given is not a 'timid grave tending life – it is adventurously expectant greeting God with a child-like: What's next?'

By the way, did you know that Josh was baptized and confirmed here? Did you know that he was born on Easter and reborn on Easter?

There's some kind of message inside that promise, too. Finally, we don't know what's on the other side of this life. Heaven isn't a place people know much about... but if there is water, I bet Josh'll figure out a way to drop a line in to it. And, if it has music, maybe he'll be 'Dancing in the moonlight' pointed finger and all.

Let's pray:
Thank you for giving Josh to us to know and to love and to laugh with for 27 years. He was a very good gift to Sammy and his family and friends and we will miss him for the rest of our lives. Help us to

remember the good times, rumble through the hard times, and to wipe the tears from our eyes when we have no words at all. Amen. Here at All Saints, we hold hands when we pray these sacred words; I encourage you to do that now.
Let's pray the prayer that Jesus taught us to pray.
Our Father, which art in heaven, Hallowed be thy Name. Thy Kingdom come. Thy will be done on earth, As it is in heaven. Give us this day our daily bread. And forgive us our trespasses, As we forgive them that trespass against us. And lead us not into temptation, But deliver us from evil. For thine is the kingdom, The power, and the glory, For ever and ever. Amen.

A Benediction literally means: good speech. But, it also is a way we share well wishes toward one another; it's a blessing.

Let all raise our right hand in a blessing toward the picture of Josh that captured him so incredibly well.
May the Lord bless you and keep you. May the Lord make his face shine upon you, and be gracious to you. May the Lord lift up his countenance upon you, and give you deep and abiding peace. In the name of the Creator, Jesus Christ, and the Holy Spirit who gives us breath and life and intercedes for us with sighs too deep for words. Amen.

Now, again, it may seem unorthodox to play a song by Pennywise for some people but the reality is that we have a ton of music that tells our story in every genre of music humankind has designed.

Josh had brothers beyond Dustin. So it's fitting that we hear the Bro Hymn as we conclude this service. Keep the stories going over at the reception or wherever you choose to go tonight. Be safe. Be kind. And: love one another.

"Bro Hymn" https://www.youtube.com/watch?v=_n8TuSVmOrw

Near the end of the service they asked a friend to sing a song by King Harvest, "Dancing in the Moonlight." https://www.youtube.com/watch?v=g5JqPxmYhlo

That was an unbearably long song. And, the person singing it started to cry. It was absolutely heart-wrenching.

After the song ended, Sammy went up to urn, picked it up, and carried it down the center aisle of the church. About half-way down the aisle she let out a guttural cry of grief like I have never heard before. It was an exclamation point at the end of a horrible tragedy. It was a sacred moment.

The family went 'left' into the dining hall. I went 'right' – right out the side door of the church. I could not hold it together any longer. I paced around the parking lot, cried, breathed, made circles with my feet, and centered myself to go to the reception. Here's the crazy aside for this night of grief, there were two dozen people crammed in the conference room for a Cheers Pablo! painting party. They were having a couple of drinks, eating snacks, and having a lovely time. What a juxtaposition!

There have been plenty of funerals where I have maintained my composure, did my job, and was able to move on to the next task at hand. To be clear, I am touched by every funeral that I attend or officiate. I am 'all in' and practice being fully present. I also recognize that the people that I am serving are not my family. This can be off-putting for some parishioners that have unwritten and unspoken expectations about the function of the pastor. It is our job to empathize with families. It is not our job to over-function and get globbed together with those who are grieving.

Globbed together may need some explanation. As you can tell, it is a highly technical term – I'm joking. Think about your own family or another family you know. Can you see where some overlapping happens? Where it is hard to tell where one person ends, and another begins because they are so close? The sort of groups of people that have a long history or herstory with one another and hardly need to use words. In the Bowen Family Systems Theory this globbed togetherness is actually called a Togetherness Force. It is a Force because 'groupthink' sets in and it is very hard to change within the system.

Pastors have their own families, which can be a blessing and a difficult reality for those who seem to need for us to enter into their pain. I have found myself in a position where family members are angry that I, in appearance, do not seem to be feeling much if anything around the death of their loved one. Creating and keeping clear boundaries has helped me to not get globbed together with the people I have been called to serve.

Now, as you read this you may be thinking, how did I pull my shit back together in order to re-enter the reception for Josh and a group of painters who were laughing full-tilt? I embodied my feelings, I let the tears roll, I allowed myself to feel all of it – the joy filled painters and the family that just wanted this night to be over: done.

Suicide sucks. It leaves families with more questions than answers. It leaves pastors in a place where we cannot explain grief and loss – nor should we. We don't have answers. We have even more questions, like: what can we do to be more emotionally intelligent, help with issues surrounding addiction, and the opioid epidemic? Mental illness is so hard to navigate! And when it ends with a death, all we can do as pastors and as human beings is show up and shut up. That in and of itself can be a sacred moment.

One more: Joey Iverson
"MINNEAPOLIS (WCCO) -- On Wednesday, a Cottage Grove family will gather to honor and remember 14-year-old Joey Iverson.
He was known at Cottage Grove Middle School as the "Adidas Kid." That's why on Wednesday, family and friends will wear their Adidas in his memory. Joey died by suicide last week.
His family is sharing their story with WCCO, with the hope it will save others.
Like many families, Joey's family spent part of last week picking out a Christmas tree. They snapped a photo of Joey and his younger sister in front of the decorated tree.
"I said oh my gosh, Joey's smiling," said Joey's sister, Lexi DuFour. "My mom said, 'I didn't even have to threaten him.' He just smiled this time and we're like he's getting better, maybe it's his season."
But this season would be Joey's last. Four hours after the photo was snapped, Joey killed himself.
"I feel like he knew deep down and he wanted to give that one last memory for his little sister," DuFour said.

DuFour says her brother started battling anxiety around the 4th grade when he developed a fear of clouds.

"That's when we were like something's really going on here," she said. "Since then, it's been a battle to try and find something that puts him at ease."

But his family says he often masked the depth of his pain with a shrewd sense of humor.

"We always said, 'You're lucky you're cute,' because he always was doing something silly and mischievous and funny," Joey's aunt Bri Beasley said.

A laugh they will forever yearn to hear again -- and a pain that many others know.

Suicide is the second leading cause of death in kids Joey's age.

"Society teaches men it's safe to be happy, it's safe to be angry, that it's not OK to be sad or afraid," said Dr. Mark Lynn, childhood psychologist at Hennepin Healthcare.

But feelings need to be felt, according to Lynn, who says parents of teens should play close attention if teens are extra withdrawn or irritable.

"There's no one risk factor; trust your gut," Lynn said. "We know all of the research and theory, but you know your child the best, and if your gut says something is wrong, you want to go in and ask the hard questions right away."

Joey's family is hoping hard questions will spare others from the hardest loss they've ever known. Lexi says she wants good to come from her dear brother's death.

"That's my goal," she said.

Lexi says she hopes to become a spokesperson for suicide prevention.

Joey's memorial service will be at 1 p.m. Wednesday at All Saints Lutheran Church. Visitation will begin at 11 a.m."

The church was packed with teens. It was my colleagues first funeral at All Saints. The therapy dog, Cooper Isaac LeRoy Yoder Erickson, made his way onto laps, nestled his head on the faces of tear-stained kids, and fell asleep during the service.

This is what we pulled together to honor Joey.

Opening

video: https://www.youtube.com/watch?v=3JKhq77ynnk&feature=youtu.be

O.A.R. - Miss You All The Time

(Opening remarks) Jules

None of us wants to be here today.

I get it.

So, I'm wondering if we can do something to start off the time we have together with an idea I learned from Brené Brown – someone who understands that humans are vulnerable, weary, and worn out.

She suggested that we give ourselves permission slips.

Permission slips to feel what we need to feel, to feel anger, sadness, frustration, anxiety – and all the happy counterparts to those I just named.

I'm giving myself permission to simply be here now, in this present moment with all of you who have gathered to say and pray your goodbyes to Joey Iverson.

A young man who touched countless lives – from women cutting hair in a beauty salon to teachers, counselors, peers, parents, siblings, aunts and uncles – his mom and dad.

It is not an easy day.

It is an important day.

It is a day to get the word out about suicide, getting help, and, what we hold as our motto at All Saints:

Do Good, Show Up, and Be Kind.

Brené Brown said in her book *Rising Strong*: "Yes, I agree with Tennyson, who wrote, " 'Tis better to have loved and lost than never to have loved at all."

But heartbreak knocks the wind out of you, and the feelings of loss and longing can make getting out of bed a monumental task. Learning to trust and lean in to love again can feel impossible."

When we love someone, our hearts break open – that's how the light gets in.

Joey cracked open hundreds of hearts, it's why we gather here today in this place, to honor him as a brother, son, cousin, nephew, grandson, friend, and child of God.

So, let's take a deep breath. Pause, and prepare to pray our goodbyes to this beautiful boy.

Now, I'll introduce to you Pastor Tanner Howard.

In the Lutheran church we have a service that is typically pretty formal.

It would not ring true to have something like that for Joey. We will not do that today.

What we will do as we gather today, is sing a song or two, hear stories and remember Joey with affection, grace, and love. We will honor and celebrate his life among us. And we will pray, and invite the Holy Spirit to dwell deeply with us here.

Today sucks. You may not feel like praying. You may not feel like singing.

You are not alone.

Know that there are professionals that can help.
Stay connected with your kids and your friends. Surround yourself with family and classmates and colleagues.
You see, that's why we gather in this place. In this church. Not because it's the place with all the answers. But because it's a place where we find God's community.
Where, when you can't pray, others will pray for you.
Where, when you can't sing, others will raise their voices.
Where, when everything seems like just too much, others will lift us up.
Sounds good?   Now, let's join in singing Amazing Grace.

A Time for Remembrances – there will be a few folks who will read / talk on behalf of the family.

Fear Is A Liar by Zach Williams, sung and played by Pastor Jules
https://www.youtube.com/watch?v=1srs1YoTVzs

Psalm 23

Homily
As much as you can: be here now. Stay with me for just a few minutes as we hear a little more about Joey.
Yes. Death is a part of being human. And, grief is one of the hardest things we'll ever do in our lives.
Back to Brené Brown: "MANIFESTO OF THE BRAVE AND BROKENHEARTED:
https://brenebrown.com/art/manifesto-of-the-brave-and-brokenhearted/

You can all rise strong. That is the promise we are reminded of today. We are not alone in our pain and our grief.

God is with us through the people around us; reminding us again and again that we are

worthwhile, capable, acceptable, and loved for free.

God is with us as we wonder about the 'why' questions of life, of death, of daily living. In fact, I'd like to invite you to consider giving up the 'why' question.

I believe Joey was not Joey when this happened.

Try to let go of the 'why' and take stock of what's going on inside of you. (pause)...

 Love deeply. Pay attention.

Celebrate Joey's life, laugh, and classic smirk in your mind's eye.

This life we have been given is not a 'timid grave tending life – it is adventurously expectant greeting God with a child-like: What's next?'

Finally, we don't know what's on the other side of this life. Heaven isn't a place people know much about...but maybe he and Cal are hanging out... who knows?

Let's pray: Thank you for giving Joey to us to know and to love and to laugh with for 14 years. He was a very good gift to his family and friends and we will miss him for the rest of our lives. Help us to remember the good times, rumble through the hard times, and to wipe the tears from our eyes when we have no words at all. Amen.

Here at All Saints, we hold hands when we pray these sacred words; I encourage you to do that now.

Let's pray the prayer that Jesus taught us to pray.

Our Father, which art in heaven, Hallowed be thy Name. Thy Kingdom come. Thy will be done on earth, as it is in heaven. Give us this day our daily bread. And forgive us our trespasses, As we forgive them that trespass against us. And lead us not into temptation, But deliver us from evil. For thine is the kingdom, The power, and the glory, For ever and ever. Amen.
Tanner:

A Benediction literally means: good speech. It is a way we share well wishes toward one another; it's a blessing.
I want to ask you to raise your right hand in a blessing toward Joey

Joey Matthew Iverson: May the Lord bless you and keep you. May the Lord make his face shine upon you with grace and mercy. May the Lord look upon you with favor, and give you deep and abiding peace. In the name of the one who gives us breath and life and hope, and who intercedes for us with sighs too deep for words - the Father, the Son, and the Holy Spirit. Amen.

We Are Called
Come, live in the light
Shine with the joy and the love of the Lord
We are called to be light for the kingdom
To live in the freedom of the city of God

We are called to act with justice
We are called to love tenderly
We are called to serve one another
To walk humbly with God

Come, open your heart
Show your mercy to all those in fear
We are called to be hope for the hopeless
So all hatred and blindness will be no more

Sing, sing a new song
Sing of that great day when all will be one
God will reign and we'll walk with each other
As sisters and brothers united in love (united in love)

We are called to act with justice
We are called to love tenderly (We are called)
We are called to serve one another
To walk humbly with God

This service was exhausting, filled with love, tears, and a firm word to be kind, always.

Chapter 5: The Mobile

Here is a case study I did on a family who lost their bearings when they lost the matriarch of the family.

-ARCH – Matri-arch / Patri-arch = Mother-Leader / Father-Leader (Chief or Ruler also applies).

I was trying to figure out why the family I was caring for was so disorganized, I mean beyond the obvious death of their beloved mother, when I realized that she was the leader of the family. In Family Systems I have learned that when the patriarch or matriarch dies there is usually a time of chaos until someone with the system assumes the role of the "-ARCH."

Most of the time the position moves by gender, at least that has been my personal observation. By that I mean from dad to son or mom to daughter. Sometimes it depends on whether the other – ARCH is 'alive and well' as to whether or not the next generation takes the position. That said, I have met many couples who have been together for a long time, have 'covered' for each other's memory issues or other physical deficits, that there is no way they could assume the –ARCH. For example, one is helping the other with all of the ADL's while the rest of the family has no idea that basic needs are not being met. For example, if Bob is covering for Jane's memory losses by prompting her or assuming all of the driving, once Bob is gone, Jane may not be able to function or even remain in the home alone.

In this case the matriarch had lived beyond her prescribed by the doctor expiration date – two years beyond. On one hand, one might think that the family would be ready to say goodbye; on the other hand, steeped in denial of the inevitable.

The eldest son is not a leader. He was dependent on his mother. The middle female child was immature and waffled over every decision. The youngest picked up the slack but had never taken the lead in any of his relationships – having three sets of kids with three different women while dating a person with borderline personality disorder. (I know – 'systems' is anti-diagnosis – in this case, knowing she had some sort of illness, kept me from physically hurting her during the funeral preparations).

It's no wonder there was disorganization. To further dissect, the husband of the matriarch has 'never made any sense' to any of the children or any of the extended family. And I quote, "Don't get me wrong, I love my dad. But my mom could have done so much better!" This statement was from the youngest; he's the one with the four children from three different women while dating the latest girlfriend.

As the three children reluctantly stepped up to offer thanks for all those who assembled for the matriarch's funeral, the daughter found the microphone first. The sons, both in their 50's, needed me to escort them to the lectern. On the way, the oldest said, "We don't know where to go because we have lost our leader." How revealing!

I'm not a real big fan of the sibling positioning as one of the concepts, I point to the fact it was adopted into the eight concepts, yet in this case it helped. Sometimes I see the positions of the siblings inside of the grief continuum and it helps me ease off their scattered and shattered hopelessness during the planning process. This concept helps me have more grace for the family. As some may not be familiar with the eight concepts of Bowen Family Systems Theory, it is important to note that Walter Toman was the person who created the theory of sibling positioning. What is helpful about the concept is that we tend to revert to the position we held within our family of origin whenever we return home or meet up with our family of origin.

What I found truly fascinating is this fact: every system needs a leader. To recognize that on what is called "The Continuum of Differentiation" is one thing, but to meet the maturity or lack of maturity that occurs when grief is fully on board is another. I know that children do not move above the level of their parents without a ton of work. If the matriarch was a 25 and the husband a 19 or 20 on the continuum of differentiation, it is likely that the children would post somewhere in-between: 22, 23. The youngest in this case held the highest. These numbers I imagined were not based on the education level of the siblings – it's just my guess because of the way they functioned within the family system.

In systems the numbers are based on the ability to define self within whatever system you are operating in. The only person that had an actual opinion was the youngest. He also had insight about the deficiencies his dad would encounter now that the matriarch was gone.

Pay attention to the –ARCH in every system you encounter. Keep a steady eye on the person who assumes the new role once they are gone. It will serve you well to take a stadium view as you serve families during particularly difficult (nodal) times of transition and change. Grief 'does a number' on any system. When systems are muddling through grief I believe that the ride gets even bumpier when the –ARCH position remains in a liminal zone. The sooner the position is filled, the better most systems can manage the journey of a new normal.

Which brings us to the heart of this chapter, the importance of the genogram as a mobile. In the chart drawn below you will see a family of origin represented by squares (men) and circles (women). The age of the children on the chart are from oldest to youngest.

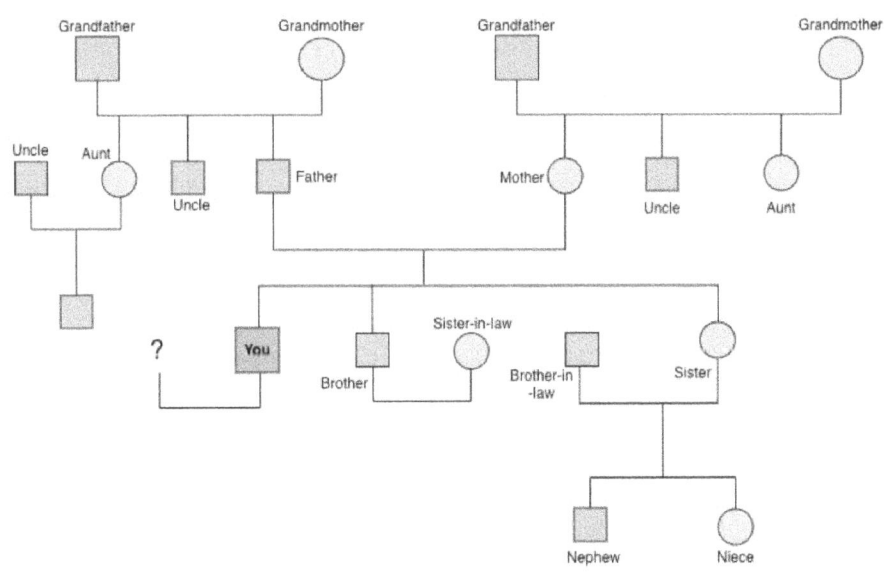

If this was an actual mobile it would be in balance, just like a safe mobile that hangs above a baby in a crib or an art installation at a modern exhibit. But if the -arch position dies, the mobile is fully out of whack. Even if one of the members of the family of origin dies, the mobile becomes unbalanced.

This leads to the question, how does the mobile become balanced again? According to the theory, it can take between five to seven years for the family system to become balanced again and that is only if someone steps into the -arch position. As in the story about the matriarch that died, 'The sons, both in their 50's, needed me to escort them to the lectern. On the way, the oldest said, "We don't know where to go because we have lost our leader."'

I've since met with one of the sons of this particular family, several times. He has stepped into the position of the patriarch but there has been quite a bit of resentment directed at him for doing so, which has resulted in him stepping back significantly. This push back is not unusual. In fact, it's quite normal. Resentment is a result of unmet expectations. How does one meet the expectations of a family if there is no mutual respect? How are expectations met if there are issues around finances, activities of daily living, or health issues that are now more acute due to the stress of the death? It makes sense that the oldest in this system has distanced himself from the rest of the family.

Is there hope for families that go through similar issues surrounding grief? You bet. I have moderated more than one family meeting following a death or an ambiguous loss. There are all sorts of professionals that can help systems 'reboot', clarify expectations, and sort through how the family members function going forward. This takes time. This takes using words. This takes a non-anxious presence and a clear agenda.

Brené Brown, Social Worker and an accomplished researcher in vulnerability within systems has a very helpful acronym that she uses when establishing trust within relationships. It's called BRAVING and you've already read about it in a previous chapter. I recommend all of her books to people that are going through major (or minor) life transitions. Above all, I recommend her book *Rising Strong*. It outlines what I mentioned in the introduction: the reckoning (the end of someone or something), the rumble (the liminal zone of uncertainty, also known as the swamp), and the revolution (the new beginning).

This is the most effective tool that I have found for building and rebuilding relationships. I have used it for staff, the congregational council, advanced leadership training, and grief classes. I use it for my own relationships, friendships, and family. The great part about the BRAVING code of living for me is that when something is off in a relationship it has helped me see both sides. Where did the train go off the tracks? What did I do or not do within these seven elements of trust?

In Brown's book, *Braving the Wilderness*, she talks about how difficult it is to enter into the messy middle. In this quote she calls it the wilderness.

Basically what she says is that when we fully belong to ourselves we are brave and we will find ourselves in a sacred place. The wilderness, by contrast, is like Yoda telling Luke Skywalker, "Into the cave you must go."

We're back to sacredness, again. Sometimes when we are grieving we feel like we don't belong anywhere. It's hard to figure out where to go, what to do, how to move on...especially when the rest of the world is moving along as if nothing has happened at all. Don't people realize that my world has ceased to exist as I know it? That is just one of the many questions that pop into the mind of someone who has had their world altered by a death, an ambiguous loss, or a major life transition.

Chapter 6: Complicated Griefs to Bear

After over two decades of leading a conversation of Grief in the Family System through KOK Funeral Services and Cremation I have learned a lot about Bowen / Friedman Family Systems Theory and how it can be applied to funerals and premarital education.

During the first part of the grief class I ask the participants to share how they ended up in a group they never wanted to join, namely, a Grief Group. Participants share their own name and then the name(s) of the people they lost. Sometimes they share how and when their person died. And, an interesting trend has been the acute loss surrounding pets. I have heard more than one person say: I loved that dog more than I have ever loved a human being.

After everyone who wants to share how they landed in the Grief Group I mention a few resources that I have found to be helpful for people as they navigate grief. Kübler-Ross wrote "On Death and Dying" many years ago. While it was one of the first books that truly resonated with people, particularly those in bereavement studies and practices, it is not research based.

From Wikipedia, the free encyclopedia:
"The Kübler-Ross model (otherwise known as the five stages of grief) postulates a progression of emotional states experienced by both terminally ill patients after diagnosis and by loved-ones after a death. The five stages are chronologically: denial, anger, bargaining, depression and acceptance.

The model was first introduced by Swiss psychiatrist Elisabeth Kübler-Ross in her 1969 book "On Death and Dying", and was inspired by her work with terminally ill patients.[1] Motivated by the lack of instruction in medical schools on the subject of death and dying, Kübler-Ross examined death and those faced with it at the University of Chicago medical school. Kübler-Ross' project evolved into a series of seminars which, along with patient interviews and previous research, became the foundation for her book.[2]

Kübler-Ross noted later in life that the stages are not a linear and predictable progression and that she regretted writing them in a way that was misunderstood.[3]"Kübler-Ross originally saw these stages as reflecting how people cope with illness and dying," observed grief researcher Kenneth J. Doka, "not as reflections of how people grieve."

I agree with Doka. I see grief having many of the five emotional stages or 'states' as recorded above but there's no order. We bounce all over the place. Our emotions are swift and more like a river with all sorts of bends – we never know what is going to happen around the next corner, will there be rapids, a quiet easy section, a waterfall, or even an alligator? Who knows. Grief is a heightened emotion that sends us clinging to our rafts for dear life.

I recommend the book *Rising Strong* by Brené Brown for several reasons. One, she echo's the understanding of what any transition looks like in a three phase approach. I'll toggle William Bridges book titled *Managing Transitions* in parentheses to expand her language and to give you a quicker understanding of each movement.

First, we have the Reckoning (The End).
Second, the Rumble (The Liminal Zone). This is the place where we need to lean in instead of running away, self-soothing, or becoming so busy that we never deal with the emotions that are a part of healing. Bridges would add that this liminal zone, from the word 'limbo', is a place where creativity and chaos live side by side.

Third, the Revolution (The New Beginning) is when we move on into the next minute, hour, day, week, month, year, decade, and so on, by creating healthy connections to others. It's a place where we reinvest ourselves in healthy and meaningful ways.

Caleb Wilde in his Confessions of a Funeral Director wrote that when we're in deep grief our brains chemistry actually changes. He said, "Grief brain is like being drunk. It's hard to be 'in the moment' as nearly 80-90% of your brain energy is being redirected to grasping the new normal of life after loss." (Page 64).

It is also important to note that grief work (and it is WORK!) is not linear. We don't follow any sort of pattern. In fact, all of our patterns have been radically disrupted and it feels like the whole world doesn't give a damn about our pain, our loss. Like I said, it's loopy, circular, spiral, or, like that river that twists and turns.

One of the tools therapists use is called a Grief Loop. Here's an illustration from eagleswingssoar.blogspot.com that sums up my point better than words can do.

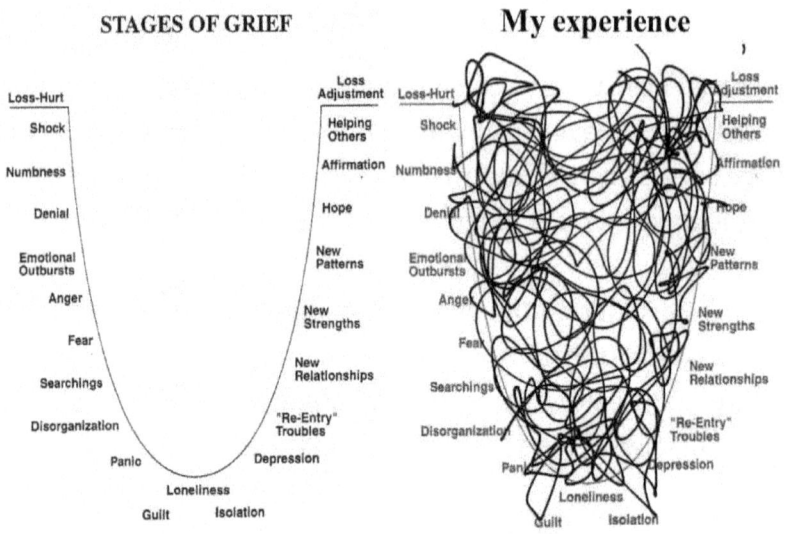

Part of the loopiness, for lack of better word, has to do with our own family system. This goes back to the previous chapter where I used the -arch and the genogram to introduce the imbalance that occurs in the hanging mobile.

This brings me to another tragic story, actually, there were two stories that ran into each other all in one day. The first was about Tonia. A parishioner, Denise, called me up and asked me to go to lunch with her. We met at Applebee's and I listened to her tell me about her best friend, Tonia, a fellow Harley biker buddy, and her instant death while on a benefit ride for another friend of their club.

Steve, her boyfriend, was still in Regions Hospital and would remain there for several months as his body was screwed and plated back together.

The accident was a result of a distracted driver who crossed the centerline of the highway.

Tonia's family belonged to a conservative protestant church in Wisconsin, which is where the funeral was held. During the actual funeral the 'pastor' stood before her biker friends and said, "If Tonia had not had this lifestyle she would still be alive now."

Pause. Breathe. Repeat.

Needless to say, there were a ton of really pissed off bikers, Denise among them. As I sat across the table from her, watching her wipe tear after tear away, I said, "Denise, do you think we can try to unring that bell and offer a service at All Saints after Steve (also known as 'Sassy' – for good reasons) gets out of the hospital? She looked relieved and agreed to help sort out the date and the nuts and bolts of the service.

A day or two after I had met with Denise (also known as 'Ma' because she is the matriarch of the Pretzel – the place where her club meets every Friday night), I went to meet with Steve. However, before I was able to see him I led a service for a woman who had been murdered by her boyfriend of 20+ years.

See the chapter titled "Complicated Grief" for more information.

When I met Sassy, he told me all about their life together. He shared sweet stories of travels, day to day meals, and the joy of finding the love of his life. In fact, he also mentioned that she curled up next to him when he was in the Emergency Room. He physically felt her presence and the kiss she placed on his cheek. Perhaps there are 'thin places' between this life and the next?

He wanted the service to be about her, not about shaming her tribe. They tribe showed up on their bikes in full leather gear, bandanas, rings, tattoos, and all the rest. Here's what I pulled together for her service:

Tonia Stocking "Nana"
Today we gather to pray our goodbyes to Tonia. We are here to support one another in our sadness and in our grief.

We are here to tell stories and to remember her, celebrate the gifts she brought into this world, and hear a word of hope in the midst of this terrible tragedy.

The first thing I want to say to you all is simple: accidents happen.

You know this, particularly because on the day Tonia was taken from us you were on a benefit ride for another friend who died on a ride.

These events were not 'consequences' of being bikers.

Accidents: happen.

We live in a world where people are distracted, not only behind the steering wheels as they 'drive' but as an entire culture.

We drown out our emotions will all sorts of distractions,
from candy crush to eating too much of the wrong kinds of food.
We soothe our weary souls by watching too many screens, hitting too many 'likes', and generally speaking: we do not pay attention to the gifts that are right around us in each present moment.

That's part of being human.

But what is also part of being human is that we get to be 'accidental saints' to each other, namely, we get to share love, and light; goodness and grace with every single person we encounter.

God did not need another 'angel'.
God did not 'call Tonia home'.

God did not want so many hearts to be sad, to be filled with so much grief.

Anne Lamott wrote in Traveling Mercies:
"You will lose someone you can't live without, and your heart will be badly broken, and the bad news is that you will never completely get over the loss of your beloved.
But this is also the good news
They live forever in your broken heart that doesn't seal back up.
And you come through.

It's like having a broken leg that never heals perfectly—that still hurts when the weather gets cold, but you learn to dance with the limp."

This will be particularly true for Steve, as it's likely he will not only have a limp for the rest of his life – he'll also learn how to dance again – physically and / or figuratively.

Following the accident, Ma, as many of you know Denise, called me up and we met for lunch.

After a long conversation about life, death, loss, and shame, I mentioned an author to her that I thought she might like.

Nadia Bolz-Weber is a heavily tattooed ELCA pastor, just like me. Nadia makes no apologies for who she is as a person.

She simply happens to be a pastor who has a good grasp on grace and has the ability to swear like a sailor.

She also creates a space in the world for people, all people, to 'fit in' no matter how they look, what club they belong to, where they worship, or what kind of bike they ride.

(I plugged in a paragraph here by Nadia Bolz-Weber that spoke about how we're super messy and life is beautiful and we don't always get it right but God loves us anyway.)

That's why we're here: to teach each other about God's love. And to be kind.

To meet people wherever they are in body, mind, and spirit.

Nadia goes on to say: *"Those most qualified to speak the gospel are those who truly know how unqualified they are to speak the gospel."* We are here to share God's amazing Grace.

All of us are children of God, which means we are loved for free, capable, acceptable, worthwhile, and NEVER ALONE.

That is the heart of the gospel that we hear about in one of the most iconic songs about God's love: Amazing Grace.

And for the gift of Tonia, and the love she brought into so many lives, we can all say: Thanks be to God. Amen.

Shortly thereafter the lighters came out and they all belted out the song: Delta Dawn. Wow. Another sacred moment.
Two years later, I officiated a double biker wedding. 'Till death do us part.' Amen.

Fast forward another two years…

The beautiful lady on the far right of the photo died of cancer.

Here's her funeral.

Denyse Espersen
June 8, 2019; 5:00p.m.

I first had the pleasure of meeting Denyse around preparation for a wedding...

Many of you may remember that I said:
"Dearly beloved We are gathered here today To get through this thing called "life" Electric word, life It means forever and that's a mighty long time But I'm here to tell you There's something else, The afterworld A world of never-ending happiness You can always see the sun, day or night..."
We're not going to talk about the afterworld – no one knows what it looks like – and, it seems only a few of know how to get there, and, by that I mean:

Show Up.
Do Good.
Be Kind.

This also sounds like what most of you do, day in and day out, as you go about your lives – or, at least you try to in an ALPHA-MALE "I got this – sort of way."

Raise your hands if you fit into that category... never-mind, I know who you are...
Ah, laughter.
That's one of my favorite things about Denyse.

I loved her laugh.
It was full, genuine, and one of the best sounds in the world.

I can still hear it as I think back to the Double Biker wedding when I said,
"When Ma asked me if I'd officiate a double biker wedding here at the Pretzel, my response was immediate: Hell ya!

Most of you might have said: Geez, it's about time."

And, then, later on, I asked: Do these Denises take these two bikers dudes to be your husbands?

They both said: Hell ya!

Now, two years later, we are thanking our sister for loving us, laughing with us, and for being a part of our lives.

This grief work is tough stuff.

I actually think that we never GET THROUGH grief; rather we absorb it.

Absorption takes time.

Take whatever time you need.
Each of you will grieve at a different pace; that's cool.

Take care of yourself.
Take care of each other.

Take care of Steve and his family, as well as the framily you guys created on the river and on the road.

Cathleen Falsani wrote:
"I keep thinking: Now she knows— All the secrets. All the answers. Every mystery. Now she sees. The whole picture. The entire story. Face to face. Now she is. Whole. Remarkable. Perfect. All of who she ever was. All of who she is. In the More. In memory. Now. Denyse picked out a few songs for her time with you all today."

The first, not even on the radar of Ma, was by Sara Bareilles, "I Choose You". If you don't know it, listen to it.

https://www.youtube.com/watch?v=xjE5D9cHiOk

Steve, man, I am so sorry.
Also, I'm so glad you two chose each other.
You were by her side through thick and thin, infusions and vacations – you got it right.

Mary Oliver wrote:
 "To pay attention, this is our endless and proper work."
You paid attention.
You listened to her needs and honored her wishes.
Thank you, thank you, thank you.

Denyse also picked out a song that most of us are still shaking our heads at… this wasn't on my radar, either, but it's an oldie but goodie:

Kansas' DUST IN THE WIND.

Stephanie did not dodge the bullet on this Memorial service…

So, bear with it as I try to hack it out on guitar and she sings it. We can both use a little support, so if you know it, sing it – we are NOT Kansas.

Sing: Dust in the Wind. (And we did it with much gusto!)

Life is short.
Love well.
Show Up.
Do Good.
Be Kind.

Stevie, you're up.

Denyse Espersen. She was such a very special person to all. She was a wonderful wife, cherished 2nd mother, a loving grandmother, a sister, and a daughter. Aside from maintaining all these roles, she always added another characteristic to your relationship …she was always your friend first.

Denyse had many friends that she loved. Whether it be her loyal friends from the Pretzel, her loving boating friends, or the co-workers she had over the years. This amazing lady could fit in most anywhere and always held her friendships very close to her heart.

Denyse had a way about her that people are drawn to. She could share so much with you just with a look. And there were a few looks...

The "I love you" look.
If you look through the photos, you will see this look a lot when she was with Dad. The look of love in her eyes could light up the entire room when she looked at Dad and vice versa when dad looked at her. You just knew that they were meant to be together.

The "Oh yeah, I saw that" look.
Denyse was very attentive to her surroundings. She would literally catch everything going on in the room around her. Even if you might not think she was paying attention, you could glance over and get a quick wink or a nod indicating "I saw that too".

And then of course - our family favorite, there was the "SLOW BLINK".
This was the look that she would give Dad when he said something she didn't like. There would usually be a quick, little sigh first, then the stare and the slow blink. This meant, "I can't believe you just said that!". It wasn't always directed at dad, he just usually said goofy things more often than the rest of us.

Denyse had such a clever mind with an amazing sense of humor. One of our favorite recent family examples was a "Christmas ornament" she made for my mom and John. Mom and John had recently lost their RV to an accidental fire. The RV was totally charred. Denyse was later out shopping and found a toy RV with a master plan. She sent a photo text to my sister stating: "Ooh, when this toy RV meets some flame, it will make a really nice Christmas ornament for your mom and John." Denyse then had Dad make a fire in the fire pit and threw the toy RV in until the wheels were melted, took it out and put a hook in the top. Perfect! It was displayed as part of a Thanksgiving centerpiece for Mom and John when they arrived for our holiday dinner. We all laughed our asses off for hours when Mom and John realized what it was. Mom and John laughed as well. Mom still has this "Christmas ornament" hanging in her kitchen window.

Our entire family will miss her more than words can describe. She helped to bring all of us together, mend any misunderstandings, and brought an amazing closeness that will forever be appreciated. She loved our Dad as much as a woman can possibly love a man and made him the happiest we've ever seen him. She truly loved us kids as her own and was always so proud to introduce us as such. She brought so much joy and happiness to all that she met. She truly loved the life that she and Dad created on 5th street. She loved it so much, and fought so hard right up until the very end. The strength and courage that she displayed was second to none. Even during her final days, she was concerned with how everybody else was doing. When you asked how she was doing, she would always say "I'm ok, how are you?". Our dearest D, we will cherish our most precious memories with you forever and ever. You may have left this earth, but you will forever be in all of our hearts. Until we meet again...

ALMIGHTY GOD, IN HOLY BAPTISM YOU HAVE KNIT YOUR CHOSEN PEOPLE TOGETHER IN ONE COMMUNION OF SAINTS, IN THE BODY OF CHRIST. GIVE TO YOUR WHOLE CHURCH IN HEAVEN AND ON

EARTH YOUR LIGHT AND YOUR PEACE. GOD OF MERCY, People: Hear our prayer.

GIVE COURAGE AND FAITH TO ALL WHO MOURN, AND A SURE AND CERTAIN HOPE IN YOUR LOVING CARE, THAT, CASTING ALL THEIR SORROW ON YOU, THEY MAY HAVE STRENGTH FOR THE DAYS AHEAD. GOD OF MERCY,

People: Hear our prayer.

GRANT TO US WHO ARE STILL IN OUR PILGRIMAGE, AND WHO WALK AS YET BY FAITH, THAT, WHERE THIS WORLD GROANS IN GRIEF AND PAIN, YOUR HOLY SPIRIT MAY LEAD US TO BEAR WITNESS TO YOUR LIGHT AND LIFE. GOD OF MERCY, GOD OF MERCY,

People: Hear our prayer.

HELP US, IN THE MIDST OF THINGS WE CANNOT UNDERSTAND, TO BELIEVE AND TRUST IN THE COMMUNION OF SAINTS, THE FORGIVENESS OF SINS, AND THE RESURRECTION TO LIFE EVERLASTING. WE PRAY, ESPECIALLY TODAY, FOR THE JIM BURDICK as he begins his first round of chemo today – and, we pray for all those who struggle with cancer and illnesses of the body, mind, and soul. GOD OF MERCY,

People: Hear our prayer.

GOD OF ALL GRACE, WE GIVE YOU THANKS BECAUSE BY HIS DEATH OUR SAVIOR JESUS CHRIST DESTROYED THE POWER OF DEATH AND BY HIS RESURRECTION HE OPENED THE KINGDOM OF HEAVEN TO ALL BELIEVERS. MAKE US CERTAIN THAT BECAUSE HE LIVES WE SHALL LIVE ALSO, AND THAT NEITHER DEATH NOR LIFE, NOR THINGS PRESENT NOR THINGS TO COME, WILL BE ABLE TO SEPARATE US FROM YOUR LOVE IN CHRIST JESUS OUR LORD, WHO LIVES AND REIGNS WITH YOU AND THE HOLY SPIRIT, ONE GOD, NOW AND FOREVER. People: Amen.

Let us pray.

Eternal God, in whose love nothing is lost: Into your hands we commit your servant Denyse, whom you have known from before she was born and held in your watchful care. As her body is changed back to the energies and elements of the earth from which it came, may she return to you to be clothed in a shining resurrection body and joined in the joyful company of all the saints in light.

Bless us who hold her in memory and cherish the good love and labor of her life. When morning comes, turn our separation into reunion and transform our grieving into joy, through Jesus Christ our Redeemer and your Holy Spirit who is the breath and fire of love, who dwells with you, one God, now and forever. Amen.

Let's join hands and hearts as we pray the prayer that Jesus taught us. (Here we prayed the Lord's Prayer).

Let's hold our right hands up in blessing:

God of Grace, we bless Denyse., whom we love and see no longer.
Grant to her eternal rest. Let light perpetual shine upon her.
May her soul and souls of all the departed, through the mercy of God, rest in peace. Amen.

The peace of the Lord be with you all!
Now, go in peace, celebrate life, and keep the stories and legacy of Denyse going.

Postlude: Four On the Floor by Lee Brice.

A few months later I was asked to preach at the chapel at Luther Seminary. I gave a summary of the sermon and how pastors can meet people where they are at.

Amen.

Chapter 7: The Queen Mum

Not to be confused with Queen Elizabeth, Gloria Thompson, the Queen Mum, was the matriarch of ASLC. She was always well put together, kind, compassionate, generous, and had a wonderful playfulness about her interior. She was a 'brittle diabetic'. Had it not been for her best friend, who happened to be a nurse, it is likely she would have died a decade before her time. The family and her bestie arranged for a magnificent send off. Here are a few of my words that I lent to the occasion.

Gloria Thompson 18 September 2017 – 11a.m. worship service. Age 83, of St. Paul Park, passed away into the loving arms of Jesus, September 11, 2017. Preceded in death by her husband, Norman. Survived by her family, best friend, Sandy Schuck, Faith Anderson (Carl), Dave (Linda), Paul, Mark (Kari); 20 grandchildren and 18 great-grandchildren; brother, Bill Johnson (Laurie) as well
as many other loving relatives and friends. Gloria was the embodiment of grace and love to all that encountered her. Leading through a Christ-like heart, she served as the cornerstone of faith to her family, as well as the congregation at All Saints Lutheran Church where she was a charter member. Her love of beauty extended out from within her into a career of managing three different department stores, Field-Schlick, Van Arsdell and Herberger's. She had a keen eye for fashion that she carried throughout her life. She loved to work in her
gardens; Gertens being a favorite spot, travel and most importantly, ice cream.
Gloria will be remembered as her name implies, full of the Glory of the Lord, always welcoming and always loving.

Her funeral homily:

The Bible passage I chose to share with you today comes from Proverbs 16:31 (NRSV)

Gray hair is a crown of glory; it is gained in a righteous life.

Gloria once hit me in the head with a marshmallow - during worship - on a holy humor Sunday.

I'll let you digest that for a second.

Gloria, proper, glorious, kind, gracious Gloria, threw a marshmallow at my head and that marshmallow found its target.

You're welcome.

Gray hair is a crown of glory - Gloria; you not only gained a righteous life, you lived it.

To be "right" is not something Gloria ever had to be - what she lived well was the word we know as "righteousness," which means to Lutheran Christians: to be in right relationship with God, with one another.

Gloria and I had many conversations about faith, family, God, and, especially: the Holy Spirit. And, Sophia, Wisdom. Beauty in all things...

As Sarayu, in The Shack.

Ruach – breathe. Repeat. The Spirit intercedes for us with sighs too deep for words to express.

This same spirit will abide with all of you as you grieve.
She will step into your sorrow, expand her wings, and wrap you up in love when words are no longer available. That is the nature of grief.

Words are not necessary in this initial grief work: presence is. Show up. Be there. Be here now. Preach the Gospel always, when necessary: use words... I could go on...Words will come along later, as we heal, write, reflect, remember and repeat, more on that as we move into the future known as the new normal...

Gloria loved this elusive aspect of the Triune God, Breath of Life. The Holy Spirit.
From dem bone, dem bones, dem dry, dry, bones - the spirit breathed life back into death in the great reversal of Ezekiel's warriors...

To "The Spirit of the Lord is upon me to declare good news to all people, the poor, the naked, the imprisoned, the hungry, the thirsty because, all means all." (Mark 2).

Jesus unfurled that roll - just as surely as 'Glory Filled Gloria' is unfurling her wings in her first home, alongside Norm, and so many people she loved.

It reminds me of the Jean Formo quote I know she loved and appreciated:

Death is God carrying us in one arm while the other flings aside heaven's door to welcome us back to the blazing hearth of our first

home, while those inside, having arrived before us rush to the door like glad children, shouting, "They're here! They're here!"
Death has a bad name on earth but in heaven, it's a homecoming party every time the door opens. God does not forget those earthbound children, sad and left behind. God leaves the party early to enter into their despair and to get them ready for their own homecomings someday."

God is entering into our despair, tell me yours: yours; I'll tell you mine.

There once was a story about a person who had been given a great sum of money, the next – a wee bit less, a third – less even still.

The first invested money like love: extravagantly: all in: with great risk.

The second in a bank – conservative, with a decent return.

The third buried it – out of fear.

We know this story of the Parable of the Talents from Matthew's gospel...
As we know, the first got the highest praise: Well done, good and faithful servant. To the second: a pat on the back; to the third: not so much. No risk, no reward.

One of the most remarkable conversations I had with Gloria occurred this last year.

I asked her if she was ready to go home. To her first home.

She said she only had one question: Did I do enough?
I said to her: More than enough! Well, done, good and faithful servant; you have been faithful in all things; now, go in peace.

Or, as Sam Baker sang:
Go in peace Go in kindness Go in love Go in faith Leave the day The day behind us Day is done Go in grace Let us go Into the dark Not afraid Not alone Let us hope By some good pleasure Safely to Arrive at home Let us hope By some good pleasure Safely to Arrive at home
I believe she has arrived safely to her first home.
And for the gift of Glory, who wore a crown of gray hair with the dignity of the Queen Mum, a righteous and beloved woman of faith, we can all say:
Thanks be to God. Amen.

We sing: You Are Mine.

Of course, that is not where the service ended, we continued with more liturgy, prayers, music, the commendation, and, many, many more blessings.

One of my favorite theologians, Dietrich Bonhoeffer, wrote,

"Nothing can make up for the absence of someone we love, and it would be wrong to try to find a substitute; we simply hold out and see it through. That sounds very hard at first, but at the same time, it is a great consolation, for the gap, as long as it remains unfilled, preserves the bond between us. It is nonsense to say God fills the gap; God does not fill it, but on the contrary, God keeps it empty, and so helps us to keep alive our former communion with each other even at the cost of pain. The dearer and richer our memories, the more difficult the separation. But gratitude eventually changes the pangs of memory into a tranquil joy. The beauties of the past are borne again, a precious gift in and of themselves."

When we love well, grief still shows up. Grief cannot be avoided. But when we love well, I believe that grief has wings. It can lift us up, move us forward, allow us to return to fond memories, and can help us heal. From songs like, "Thy Holy Wings" to "You Raise Me Up" we are reminded that death, again, does not have the last word. We are not alone in our sadness. We do not have to fill the gap. We simply get to recognize it for what it is, take a deep breath, and move into a new adventure.

Chapter 8: The Matriarch Died

Betty died in 2000. Betty was my partner's mom. She was the matriarch of the family system. There is much to say about Betty and Beth and the "Finnish Mafia" as I tend to refer to my wife's family, but I will refrain from our own experience of loss and grief for a moment to share an insight about leadership within the family system.

Back to Betty. Because she was the glue that held the family together and was a well-differentiated leader as a parent, her death had a huge impact on the entire clan, but particularly upon the youngest son.

Now, to be clear, I was reluctant to share this story because it was incredibly hurtful to me and to Beth, but Beth insisted. The reality is, this story is important because sometimes people act like assholes when they are hurting.

Beth took FMLA for several months leading up to Betty's death. As the only daughter she saw this time with her mother as a duty and a delight, a privilege and a challenge. After Betty died, I drove up to Esko to be with Beth for the wake and the funeral. This did not bode well with Charlie.

To be completely honest, I do not remember exactly what he said to me word for word. I do remember thinking that I wanted to punch him in the nose. His basic sentiment was: How dare you show up here during our time of loss?

Now, looking back, Charlie was being cruel, to be true, but he was also grieving. This is where, twenty years later, I can see that he lashed out at me because I'd stepped into his territory, he didn't know that the territory was also mine. Charlie and I did resolve our differences over time. It took a long time.

Here's a little context. Beth and I have been together since 1995. The faith tradition she was raised in was even more conservative than the one I was raised in. Both of our family systems were seated in white male privilege from the pulpit to the doctrinal foundations of both the LCMS and the Finnish Apostolic Lutheran Church. This common conservative thinking bonded us deeply.

We have both left those traditions and have sought what this quote sums up about church and life in community. "Christianity did not begin with a confession. It began with an invitation into friendship, into creating a new community, into forming relationships based on love and service."

Our life together is based on love and service. Love and service toward each other, our relationship with God, and, our family systems, even when our families of origin choose doctrine over relationship. We wrote a Ketubah when we first decided to make a lifelong commitment to one another. In 2014 we were able to publicly enter into matrimony. The ELCA had changed its understanding on gay marriage and the state and country soon followed.

It's important to recognize the values we wrote all those years ago were still consistent with the values we still hold deeply to each and every day. The piece that is so interesting for us is that we were dedicated to right relationships within our family of origins.

Here's the Ketubah in its original form that we had read at our marriage ceremony.

Covenant of Partnership between
Beth & Jules Erickson

It is with honor of our relationship with God and with one another that we recognize that we have been given to one another as a gift, and therefore share with each other this ketubah.

(A ketubah כ.תוּבּ.ה; is a document which outlines the rights and responsibilities of each person in the covenant agreement.)

We will treat one another every day as if it were our last day together.
We will trust one another during the maturing process of our relationship; we will treat each other with respect and dignity.
We will work on our relationship as if our lives depend upon it.
We will not expect each other to fulfill all of our needs.
We will surround ourselves with systems that are consistent with our values.
We will speak words that remind each other how much we treasure, cherish, adore, and love each other each and every day.
We will join in the art of reciprocity and name our individual needs in all areas of our relationship.
We will be tender and gentle with each other.
We will continue to speak of God and learn about God together and apart.

We will make time to play together, to laugh, and to enjoy God's good gifts, including one another and the communities we serve.
We will pray for wisdom, especially when it relates to the future of our nieces, nephews, and extended families.
This is our life together. Our ketubah reflects what we hope to live out as partners in service to one another – in good times and in difficult times.
Amen.
This covenant agreement informs how we understand our interactions with all people, as well as how we treat each other.

I'm including this Ketubah and the death of Betty in this book because, in this system, I was not Beth's wife. I was not allowed to sit with her. This is one more type of 'grief'.

There are all sorts of ways that we look at grief. I added this section to this chapter because my family of origin and Beth's family of origin gave us a baseline for our faith.

Tragic grief is an extension of Complicated Grief because it has to do with mental illness and our feeble attempts to thwart it in the lives of people we love. It's also super messy because we tend to discharge blame on innocent bystanders.

Case studies:
The death of a highly anxious boy who was being treated for depression and anxiety only to have cyber bullies tell him to 'go kill himself', so he did.
The ongoing betrayal of a former pastor who is serving time for cyber crimes against children from the parish he served.

Nieces and nephews who cannot come out to their family because they are in a similar parallel universe to the Bat-Shit-Crazy-Right Wing-Evangelical Church – where praying away the gay or lesbian isn't good enough – one has to repent in front of the Elders in order to receive good standing in community.

In many of these stories there is a harsh reality of relief that goes right alongside death. I have been around families that have been holding their breath for years, desiring healing for their children, only to have it end in death by suicide.

It's not just complicated: it is tragic.

Part of me wonders what we can be doing as leaders in the free world to diminish mental illness and the bullying from what I call 'the cheap seats'. The 'Cheap Seats' are the critics who make horrendous statements online, like: go kill yourself, to the weakened ones of society.

There's also a big piece of me that wants to send out the message of Murry Bowen by way of Ed Friedman in *A Failure of Nerve* concerning what defines us and what does not. I've been marinating in Chapter 4 of the book mentioned and believe it makes sense. However, I also foresee that very few people are willing to 'Go Home' and sort out the important stories of our Family of Origin. Not only that, but we tend to sanitize those stories in such a way that our memory has been tainted.

Nostalgia, as we talked about in a recent System's Seminar for Clergy, means 'the pain of returning home.' However, if we do not 'return home' and choose 'cut off' or 'distancing' – both terms that are self-explanatory, we cannot heal. In the same vein I wonder, if returning home is too painful or too dangerous, what can we do instead?

Write. Talk. Lament. Get it out of your being and ask the question: Is that actually true? Over and over and over and over again. Get curious. There are things that happen during periods of heightened anxiety that skew our memory. Ask family questions. Don't blame. Never shame. Wonder. Take a break. Then do it all over again.

I remember when I was trying to figure out the design of my sexuality during the latter years of high school and throughout college. In the late 1980's it was still dangerous to be GBLTQ or any of the other letters that land on the spectrum of human expression of love for self or other. I was angry. I told my parents I had a horrible childhood. I was terrified. I said things that were not true because I was frightened of the truth and believed it could not set me free.

After many years of healing I discovered that, in reality, I was adored as a child. I was moody as a teen. I was an anxious mess as a college student. And, I was sorted out after I was ordained – even though, back in 1996, I was not 'allowed' to have a partner. I could be gay but not be 'with' anyone.

We stayed in the sacristy of the church for a long time. Too long for many colleagues, not long enough for many in the family system. This, too, is a complicated grief. Thank goodness it did not end tragically.

Through all of the really hard times, Beth and I stayed the course. We stood side by side and abided with those who were uncomfortable and those who simply could not understand. Now, we have relationships with those who are our kin, at least for the most part. Some still refuse to find that God has a bigger design for human companionship than a few scary and ill-translated words in the Bible.

I ran across a song that reminded me of what it was like to have good courage.

"The Village" by Wrabel.
https://www.youtube.com/watch?v=tilsrO-3gcQ

While there are still many, many things wrong with the village, it has been our intention to be a safe place to land for those who experience the continuum of loss. It has been our duty and delight to harbor friends during difficult life transitions.

In 2020 we acquired a Statement of Welcome that is on the wall where we share meals. You can find a link to the statement here:
https://lindsayletters.co/products/you-are-welcome-here-canvas

Here's the note on the website from Lindsay:
"I was thinking about my church specifically when I wrote these words, but I also believe with all my heart that this reflects the heart of God for His Church. EVERYONE is welcome. Not one of us more than another. In Jesus' name!"

Chapter 9: Tragic Grief - A Murder and death of Two
Ramona Turner
Age 54
Saint Paul
September 17, 2015

On September 17, 54-year-old Ramona "Mona" Turner, was shot and killed by 56-year-old John "Jack" Gordon Weisner Jr., her partner of over 40 years, in their Saint Paul home. Jack Weisner then stabbed himself several times in an attempt to commit suicide. According to family, Mona had been attempting to leave the relationship for the last five years. Jack assaulted Mona in 2009 which resulted in a misdemeanor domestic assault conviction. She reported the abuse to law enforcement and her family, and sought an Order for Protection against him at that time. According to media reports, there were several instances of Weisner controlling Mona and perpetrating abuse against her. Mona, who had two sons with Weisner, was killed in the presence of one of her sons and his girlfriend.
https://www.vfmn.org/we-remember-2015

Preliminary comments from Pastor Jules:

I'm not even sure how I ended up serving as an officiant for this funeral on the East Side of St. Paul but it's not unusual for a funeral home to call around to local parishes to see if a pastor can help after a murder and attempted suicide. What I do remember, prior to the service, was sitting around with the funeral directors and eating lunch before starting the service for 'Mona'. I was reading the newspaper article about the details listed above concerning her death when one of the funeral directors said, "You know, Pastor, working on the east side is a trip. Since I started here I started carrying a gun, I have a conceal and carry license. Most of these calls, especially the ones after dark, we get in and get out. Thankfully I haven't had to use my weapon yet."

Sigh. As I usually say after such statements, as I retell them to friends and colleagues, "So that happened." Bleh.

The service for Ramona, "Mona", was packed. It was the fall of 2015 and the funeral home had every room open for overflow. I met with the two sons and their partners, expressed my support, and gave them the outline for the funeral. They were still in shock and looked exhausted.

Most of the people in attendance were casually dressed, the majority of them were wearing baseball caps or bandanas. One couple, near the front right, were wearing dress clothes, a suit and tie for the man, a lovely, conservative dress for the woman.

Here's what I said as I addressed those assembled.

Good afternoon.

My name is Jules Erickson and I am one of the pastors at All Saints in Cottage Grove.

None of us wants to be here today.

In fact, my guess is that many of us are still in shock about what happened to Mona and we may be wondering, 'what will happen next.'

So today we will pray our goodbyes, we will hear from a couple of people, and we will name what happened in a way that is truthful and respectful to this family.

Because today we recognize that John and Joshua did not lose one parent this last week, they lost two. "Jack" is also lost to this family because of his actions on September 17, 2015.

Mona is the 21st woman or child that has been murdered in domestic violence in 2015.

We all need to be a part of changing those statistics. I imagine that the majority of you never thought you would be a witness to a tragedy like this so close to your home and your hearts.

What can we do? If you are in a place where you feel as if you are in danger there are places that can help. In the back of the room there is a table set up with brochures about domestic violence along with phone numbers you can call for additional information. Especially now, I think it is important to advocate for those who may be in danger from a partner or family member. If you are in that position, please ask for help.

Now, let's take a moment to breathe in, breathe out, and prepare our hearts to comfort one another in our grief.

In the Lutheran tradition which I am a part of, we use a formal funeral format to guide us through our loss. Today, we are going to make that a lot more simple and offer a prayer or two, a psalm, and a remembrance or two.

Let us pray.
Creator God, Thank you for giving Mona to us to know and to love. She was a very good gift to this family and all who have gathered. We will miss her for the rest of our lives. Help us to remember the good times, rumble through the hard times, and to wipe the tears from our eyes when we have no words at all. Amen.

Psalm 23
A Poem from the family
A Time for Remembrance

From Romans 8:39 we hear these good words:
I'm absolutely convinced that nothing—nothing living or dead, angelic or demonic, today or tomorrow, high or low, thinkable or unthinkable—absolutely nothing can get between us and God's love because of the way that Jesus our Master has embraced us. (The Message version).

Friends and family of Mona, nothing can separate us from God's love, even when we experience the anguish of the last week or more. Take care of each other. Be kind and gentle with one another. Walk side by side with each other. If you need help, we can help. If you need to cry, cry. Feel whatever you need to feel because this is complex and exhausting. You do not have to go it alone, you were never meant to.

Let's pray the prayer that Jesus taught us to pray.
Our Father, which art in heaven, Hallowed be thy Name. Thy Kingdom come. Thy will be done on earth, as it is in heaven. Give us this day our daily bread. And forgive us our trespasses, As we forgive them that trespass against us. And lead us not into temptation, But deliver us from evil. For thine is the kingdom, The power, and the glory, For ever and ever. Amen.

A Benediction literally means: good speech. It is a way we share well wishes toward one another; it's a blessing.
Please raise your right hand in a blessing toward Mona.
Mona: May the Lord bless you and keep you. May the Lord make his face shine upon you with grace and mercy. May the Lord look upon you with favor, and give you deep and abiding peace. In the name of the one who gives us breath and life and hope, and who intercedes for us with sighs too deep for words - the Father, the Son, and the Holy Spirit. Amen.

Let us go in peace and share a sign of God's deep and abiding peace with one another. Amen.

Chapter 10: 20 Years Ordained, written December 15, 2017 - a reflection on betrayal

Every year I sit down on the anniversary of my ordination and I think about God, the church, this life, the life-style of being a pastor, if I still want to do this gig, and how I feel about the place where I serve.

What do I think about God?

God is way bigger now than 20 years ago: God is everywhere, in every religion, every person, and in everything that lives and breathes; maybe even in rocks, too. Who knows? I've taken up the idea that we know as much about God as the snail on the side of the Mississippi knows about the speedboat that just went whizzing by.

I know I've given up certainty. Also: being orthodox, in any way. By that I mean: smells and bells, pomp and circumstance. I still like liturgy because it gives worship a sense of purpose, direction, and worship to the Creator of the Universe. God does not live in heaven, some light years away. God seems to be the space between us, the Breath within us, (maybe even between us) the Sophia Wisdom that keeps us grounded, and perhaps: eudaimonia.

Liz Gilbert wrote,
"In ancient Greek, the word for the highest degree of human happiness is eudaimonia, which basically means "well-daemoned" – that is, nicely taken care of by some external divine creative spirit

guide. (Modern commentators, perhaps uncomfortable with this sense of divine mystery, simply call it "flow" or "being in the zone.")

But the Greeks and the Romans both believed in the idea of an external daemon of creativity – a sort of house elf, if you will, who lived within the walls of your home and who sometimes aided you in your labors. The Romans had a specific term for that helpful elf. They called you genius – your guardian deity, the conduit of your inspiration. Which is to say, the Romans didn't believe that an exceptionally gifted person was a genius; they believed that an exceptionally gifted person had a genius."

What do I think about church?

Here's my new bio for the website: The Rev. Dr. Jules Erickson serves as Senior Pastor, and has been with All Saints since 2003. Her ministry is focused on helping people live healthy, happy, non-anxious, and well-balanced lives. She enjoys laughing, preaching, teaching, Crossfit, good food, and people of every age (especially giggly babies). Pastor Jules and her beloved, Beth, live in Hastings with three bouncing Goldendoodle dogs.

I like to help people. I think the church is a tribe of people who are all 'just walking each other home' like Rumi said. I have no tolerance for judgmental people, negativity, and idle chatter. Instead of talking: do something. Ministry means show up: shut up. Do. Be. Be here now. You are here. That's what I think about church.

This life.

What an incredible life this is; had you told me that life as a pastor would be this intense, rewarding, terrifying, wonderful, and wild…20 years ago I might have said: shut up! I don't regret a day of it: any of it. Sure, I wish I would have curbed some words over the last 20 years but I also know that making mistakes and saying stupid shit is part of being human. I'm not going to beat myself up about past failings. I'm more of the mindset of S. Jean Ekern, a recent Saint who died well, who often said: Sure, Why Not? I've adopted that mindset, too. This life is wide open, filled with possibility and hope, darkness and light, goldendoodles and good friends that fill me with joy, grief, a sense of peace, and an ever-present reminder that I am not alone.

The Life-Style of Being A Pastor

People still say that being gay is a lifestyle. I know, shocking. A life-style is how you live your life, not with whom you abide with in matrimony. Have you ever heard a heterosexual say: I'm really into this heterosexual life-style? No. Because we choose how we live. I work hard, play hard, work out hard, sleep hard, write – every day, read – as much as I can, and limit my screen time because I learn visually and I retain almost every image I see.

Even if you have really good boundaries you are never really 'off' the clock as a pastor. While I believe I am not 'defined' as 'pastor' it is a large part of who I am as a person. There are some pastors out there that cannot 'turn off' – it's as if once they take off the collar they have no idea who they are as a person.

I feel like I've reversed that over the years. I am 'Just Jules' who happens to be a pastor. I love this vocation. I get it. I love community building. I love projects. I love people, especially babies – primarily because I hold them until they cry and then I can give them back to their parents. I love baptisms because it's God saying: I love you to kiddos through words and water. I just get to hold them and tell them they are loved for free. What a gift!

Back to life-style...it's how I spend my time: loving, caring, serving, listening, feeling, wondering, wandering, then doing it all over again. Gay or not: it's a sweet gig.

Do I still want to do this gig?

Hell yeah! I just went through the biggest shit storm in my 'ordained life' and I'm all in. I've buried pederasts who committed suicide, whose family wanted me to say it was an 'accident' and I named it what it was anyway. I buried an eleven-year-old, shy one-week of her 12th birthday, two weeks before Christmas. She hung herself in the basement of her home. I have held the lifeless bodies of babies in the hollow of my hand. I have spoken at funerals where the decedent was despicable and no one had any words of kindness. I've seen more than I ever imagined I would and I'm grateful for nearly all of it.

I have married hundreds of couples – now: same-sex and transgendered. While I'm not crazy about performing weddings, I am also grateful to do ALL weddings: legally. We'll see how long that lasts.

Again: I am all in. This has been one of the most remarkable, unique, random 'jobs' I have ever been a part of in my life. When I get tackled by a 3 year old named Trygve on a Wednesday night: I'm in, all in. 20 years ago Josh Rupprecht slammed into me from his baptism on up. I went to his graduation 3 years ago. He's a junior in college now. Another kiddo I confirmed has been ordained for nearly a decade. I love watching people throughout their entire life be a part of something bigger, an ubuntu, a family. It gives me hope, joy, and a sense that the world will survive and thrive even when the chips are down.

How do I feel about All Saints Lutheran Church, ELCA?
I feel so sad for all of the people in our little community. We've been through the wringer and it will not be over, the 'case' won't be over, for a very long time. Am I supposed to be here now? Yep. No doubt. But that said, things can change, perceptions can get twisted, and rumors still have power. I had hoped to retire from this place of grace; now: we'll wait and see. I'm open to whatever the congregation needs. If that means I have to leave: I'll go. For now I feel a little bit like the glue that's holding our shattered hearts together – at least to a certain extent. Who knows? I only have my perception and those are not always accurate.

This year, during our shit storm known as the 'Great Perversion of our Children by the associate pastor...' okay, I just made that up; this year we've gone through hell and back and I don't even believe in hell. Backstory, we default to hero, victim, or learner. I did my best to not be the hero. I had been victimized. I need to learn: alongside. That's what I have striven to do. I will continue to do just that: abide.

Some sort of house elf showed up throughout our shit storm and helped me write some divinely inspired words that helped us become sticks in a bundle through the fear, pain, and sadness we felt individually and as a community, a tribe.

All of this said, I will say: all the learning, leaning into hard places, spaces, people, and being open to pretty much anything prepared me for the moment when I had to be a person who was willing to Rise Strong. (See Brené Brown's book: *Rising Strong*).

I got the loveliest note from an old classmate, Alie Whitney Shane. She wrote simply, beautifully: thank you for being.
My dear Jules,
My heart breaks for you and your congregation. But Jules, if I were going through that evil, there's nobody I would want by my side more than you. I could go on, but for now I will leave it with this: I love you. We are with you.
Peace to you,
Love,
Alison

I baptized her daughter, Emily, before I was ordained; somehow they got a special dispensation for me to perform the sacrament. I'm Emily's god-mom. Back 21 years ago when the gays couldn't be pastors: Kent and Alison believed I would be one even if the church said: no. And, the church said: no, a lot.

But I'm still here. Doing. Being. Loving. Creating. Wondering. Failing. Celebrating. All of it.

I wonder what 2017 will bring?
Let's wait and see together.

That's where I'll leave it on the 20th year of my day of ordination.

Chapter 11: Funerals vs Weddings

Ask a pastor if they would rather do a wedding or a funeral and 9 out of a 10 times you will hear the word: 'funeral.' The general public is stunned when they first hear pastors prefer funerals to weddings in a ratio that sounds like an advertisement for Trident chewing gum. There are various reasons pastors will want to perform a funeral over a wedding. Some pastors believe that people are much more receptive to the message of hope that Christ offers through his own death and resurrection than they are at a wedding. Others see it as a wonderful outreach tool to those who have been away for a while or are what they call 'unchurched.' For me, I agree with both of the aforementioned sentiments. However, the reason I like funerals is because there is less drama and therefore more worship.

Joyce Rupp wrote a book concerning grief several years ago entitled *Praying Our Goodbyes*. That is what we do when we "Witness the Resurrection." We pray out our grief, we sing our songs of faith, we cry, we laugh, we remember. Notice that I did not say that there is less emotion at a funeral, usually there is just less drama. Unless, there are unresolved feelings within the family system, when that happens there ought to be seatbelts in the pews. I once witnessed a funeral where a son got into the lectern and blasted his dead mother with both barrels. She had been through treatment at least half a dozen times for alcohol addiction. In her final week of life she bled out. It was a brutal and horrible death, and from his perspective, a horrible life. A funeral is not the place to work such emotions out, obviously. I was not 'running' the service for this woman - but it taught me an important lesson about funerals: screen who is going to speak as if you were a government agency that uses three letter acronyms. The guidelines I use are pretty simple: (and likely not limited to my seven points listed here)

1) Ask the family to present someone who might be willing to talk about the outstanding characteristics of the beloved one.
2) Pre-read the one page document that they prepared for the eulogy prior to the funeral.
3) Make sure that they know the time limit for said eulogy. I recommend no more than five minutes.
4) Never open up the invitation to the assembly. You can still make it 'look' like the tributes are informal by setting them up in order of their material they wish to share, but do not say, "Anyone? Anyone? Bueller ?"
5) Limit it to three eulogies. Any more than that and you have echoes of an Irish Wake without the whiskey.
6) Teach them how to use the microphone without mangling the sound system.
7) Remind them to do just one thing on their way up to the podium: "Don't trip." It takes their mind off of the emotional part of the speech when they are worrying that they might just trip in front of the masses.It is indeed a privilege to 'escort people to heaven's gate' - but the other thing I've learned about funerals is that the pastor should never talk about their own grief - not of their grief for the decedent, but especially not about their own experience of grief. It comes off as arrogant, condescending, and trying - to - hard.

Along that same vein, which once again could be another chapter: Remember, preacher, you can preach about your scars (not recommended at a funeral) but never your open wounds. (See next chapter on Why Empathetic Preaching is a Bad Idea).

The gospel message is Roman's 6th period. Look it up. Memorize it. Breathe it in so deeply that it becomes a part of you. In the words of Eugene Peterson, author of a really fun and understandable translation of the Bible called The Message and another book about how to use the Bible titled *Eat This Book*, Peterson recommends that we 'HAGAH' the words. Basically what he suggests is that one chews on the words as if they are a big juicy bone in which you are intent on pulling all the marrow out of in a deeply satisfying way. What I believe people are looking for when they come to a funeral is hope. Hope, not just for the person they have come to remember, but hope for their own future life in this life and the afterlife. This is found, more often than not, in the community. Also, what surprises me again and again about funerals is that many people in attendance are experiencing grief for the first time. And, if not for the first time, many are remembering their own grief and working through their loss in yet another context.I was surprised to hear at a recent continuing education event this idea: "All counseling is grief work." Still, the more I ponder that thought, the more I agree.

At the root of many fears, compounded anger, deep hurt, and the like - one will find a goldmine filled with grief. How does a person let go of a deep loss? How do we move through the stages of grief? How do we know when we are moving through grief in such a way that we can begin to have hope once again? I could give bullet point answers to all the above in this order: gratitude for their life, you don't - the stages spin around you until you're tired of the vertigo, you start looking forward instead of looking back. Each could be their own chapter. My experience with grief is just that: you have to experience it fully. Grief is not something that you can run away from. If you try to run away from it, grief is likely to tackle you out of nowhere and pound the snot right out of you. That is the way it works. I'm not trying to be gross about it, I'm trying to express the importance of fully entering into those dark, sad, and depressing places in order that you might (eventually) receive a glimpse of new life. (Again, why I appreciate Romans 6).

Funerals... they are a ritual that helps us move through our personal and corporate grief in a safe and honoring community - when they are done right. Trust me, I've been to some that were not only done 'wrong' they were detrimental to the healing process of the whole.

As a pastor I believe it is absolutely essential to help people 'pray their goodbyes' without our own grief getting in the way. It is an honor, a privilege, and one of the great joys of serving as God's hands and feet in the world. Also, I think that some of the work we do in and around funerals falls under the definition of pastoral care that one of my mentors suggested during my internship; he said, 'Pastoral care sometimes means that you are simply supposed to 'show up and shut up.' By that I understand that it's not what we say, rather it is the ministry of presence.

But that's another chapter... The next page is my take on what NOT to do as a preacher at a funeral.

Chapter 12: Why Empathetic Preaching is a Bad Idea
by the Rev. Dr. Jules Erickson. Written 2015, edited 2021.

A few years ago I attended a funeral for a parishioner's parent. The pastor was warm and inviting as she welcomed us into the sacred space to pray, mourn, and sing together in celebration of a life well lived. When she got up to preach she told a story about her own loss, I believe it was the death of her mother. As I listened I decided, at that moment, to never preach about my own loss within the context of a funeral. I believe pastors are called to preach the good news of Jesus' death and resurrection every time we get into the pulpit. I also believe we are invited to preach our scars – not our open wounds. This leads me to the topic at hand: empathy.

In *A Failure of Nerve* by Edwin H. Friedman I read the following: (page 136)
"The word empathy is used so often today by teachers, parents, healers, and managers that few realize it only entered the English language in the twentieth century (compared to sympathy, which is four hundred fifty years old, and compassion, which goes back to 1340). According to the Oxford English Dictionary the word empathy was first employed in 1922, when a need arose to translate a German word in the field of aesthetic (einfurlant, "to feel in"). The original intent of the word empathy was to convey how projecting oneself into a work of art (painting, sculpture, theater) would enable a viewer to better appreciate the creation of being observed. In fact, the word empathy does not appear in the original edition of the Oxford English Dictionary published in 1931 after fifty years of painstaking research into the breadth and

particulars of the tongue (without the aid of word processors). The first editors were either unaware of empathy or thought it too rarified, too new, or too technical to include it...

I believe that the increasing popularity of empathy over the past few decades is symptomatic of the herding/togetherness force characteristic of an anxious society. And I say this knowing that empathy has achieved such inviolable, holy status in the thinking of some that to even question its value will be considered as irreverent, if not sacrilegious, as denying the Trinity or cursing the Land of Israel."

In our culture today there is an emphasis on being empathetic over and above being responsible. As a leader, a leader who happens to have breasts and ovaries, I am often looked upon as being distant or a 'bitch' when I encourage responsibility within the context of an emotional conversation. What I mean by that is best expressed by two quick examples.

A seminary student, who is a parishioner, calls me at home around 8:00 pm. on a Monday night. I am working on a lesson plan for a Wednesday night class. The person explains their anxiety; I listen, I ask questions, and I recommend that they sort out what the issue is with pen and paper. I clarify that I need to complete a project and say we'll follow up in the morning (as we were going to meet in a text study on Tuesday morning). The person came into my office and told me they were really 'pissed off'. I 'blew them off'. I didn't 'listen' the way they wanted me to listen. I apologized for not being able to read their mind, told them of the project deadline, explained that I was their pastor – not their therapist or friend, and recommended therapy. That sounds harsh, sounds like I was being a 'bitch', doesn't it? Well, it was softer than black words on white paper can convey. The conversation ended with clarity, a plan, and the person taking responsibility for their feelings instead of blaming me for not being able to read their mind. Two days later: an apology, a thank you.

The second story is even shorter. My colleague calls in sick to work (a rarity) but alludes to the office manager that confirmation may be cancelled. He doesn't call back to tell us one way or the other. We call him at home, wake him up, and ask, "Is there confirmation?" There was, and someone was handling it. We wished him well and signed off. The conversation was about following up in an area for which he was responsible. It was not overt concern about how he was feeling or the details of his physical ailment. Some might say I was not as empathetic as I could have been. I say, clarity concerning a program that affects close to seventy five people, including parents who drop off and pick up children, trumps gooey platitudes of well wishes. I know when I'm sick I don't want to be soothed over the phone; I want to sleep. I'll tell you what you need to know and go back to bed.

If compassion is over 700 years old, sympathy 450, and empathy less than 100, it makes me wonder why empathy is such a good thing. Which leads me to a short digression. Did you know that the word 'pederasty' gets translated into 'homosexuality', and that pederasty means inappropriate sexual power over a child? The word homosexual is less than 100 years old – which makes me wonder, what if the KJV had actually been translated from German, from the Greek, from the Aramaic, from the Hebrew, from Acadian, err – from God? Or, at least people who think they can be scribes for God in the first place. I can tell you: fag's, lesbo's, queers would not be persecuted by the zealots who do not know how to read the original language in the first place and make assumptions.

Second short digression, from a story I heard a while ago: Why does grandma cut off the ends of the ham? Because her mom did. Why did her mom cut off the ends of the ham? Because she did not have a pan big enough to cook it. We pass our indoctrination of bad theology down from generation to generation without finding out the why, even when it subjugates and negates real people. (That's another article that in the works titled 'Indoctrination' – not to be sung like Rod Stewart's 'Infatuation' – although you could if you really wanted to.)

Back to empathy. Therapists differ with systems practitioners over the word 'empathetic'. I was trying to explain to my own partner (a LiCSW) why I thought 'empathy' was a bad idea. My point was that when we over empathize with another we lose who we are and get absorbed into the other. In other words, because I am trying so desperately to relate to how you feel I will lose a part of me and absorb into you. The result is: I do not know where I end and the other person begins. If Bowen Family System Theory is primarily about being clearly defined as individuals then why blur the edges by being empathetic within the framework Friedman has laid out in his book *Failure of Nerve*?

One reason I think people like to show empathy towards people who are highly anxious is because 'empathy' seems to quell the anxiety within the system. In fact, it may calm it on the surface, but what's going on beneath the pseudo-calm? Dependence? The nurturing of a cell that cannot regulate itself and therefore must absorb into another in order to simply function? That is the essence of a non-differentiated being. To define self does not mean you do not care for them; it simply helps the boundary to be visible between entities. One reason why I think pastors have a default position to empathize with parishioners is because they have become accustomed to the role of the overfunctioner. The overfunctioner can end up feeling messianic; a savior to those they serve. Pastors like to help people heal. We're called 'wounded healers' in so many pastoral care books that it becomes nauseating. Also, pastors are not in the 'salvation' business. We are here to help people realize that the 'work' of salvation has already been done, period.

Let's look at Friedman again. (137).
"On the one hand, there can be no question that the notion of feeling for others, caring for others, identifying with others, being responsive to others, and perhaps even sharing their pain exquisitely or excruciatingly is heartfelt, humanitarian, highly spiritual, and an essential component in a leader's response repertoire. But it has rarely been my experience that being sensitive to others will enable those "others" to be more self-aware, that being more "understanding" of others causes them to mature, or that appreciating the plight of others will make them more responsible for their being, their condition, or their destiny.
It is possible, of course, to define empathy in a way that tries to nullify these effects, but I am concerned here not with the "true" meaning of the word empathy but with its use, and thus with what it has come to mean. As understood today, empathy may be a luxury afforded only to those who do not have to make tough

decisions. For "tough decisions" are decisions the consequence of which will be painful to others (although not harmful to others – an important distinction). The focus on "need fulfillment" that so often accompanies an emphasis on empathy leaves out the possibility that what another many really "need" (in order to become more responsible) is not to have their needs fulfilled. Indeed, it is not even clear that feeling for others is a more caring stance (or even a more ethical stance) than challenging them to take responsibility for themselves. As mentioned earlier, increasing one's threshold for another's pain (which is necessary before one can challenge them) is often the only way the other will become motivated to increase their own threshold, thus becoming better equipped to face the challenges of life." (136-137).

Pastors/Rabbis/Priests are to parishioners as parents are to children. It's the strange reality of the role of serving a community of faith that we are placed in that sort of a relationship, yet it is true. There is a necessary 'being set apart' from the people we are called to serve. Look at a parent that wants only to be their child's 'friend' and you will likely find a teen that cannot think for self or depends so heavily upon the parent that they are incapable of defining self.

Our call is to be like a parent. A parent needs to be able to set limits. A parent's job is to teach children responsibility. Again, these words may seem really harsh primarily because there has been no mention about love thus far. I've been running under the assumption that having children is likened to Elizabeth Stone's quote, "Making the decision to have a child is momentous. It is to decide forever to have your heart go walking around outside your body" (even if they are within the realm of the pastor to parishioner). Love is a given in this essay.

As pastors we are called to love all of our parishioners; we are called to show compassion to those we have been called to care for and nurture. We are not called to empathize so far down the rabbit hole that people do not understand what the hell we're talking about.

I knew a pastor that would drop everything to 'do' pastoral care. As a result, when he left the parish, they were literally 'like sheep without a shepherd.' And, he did a HUGE disservice to the next pastor; the expectations were so high for the new pastor that she nearly got burnt out after six months. It is irresponsible to create a dependency within any context but especially within the context of a parish.

While I do my best to 'love' the people I have been called to serve – it is clear that I have favorites. I cannot help that and I will not apologize for being human. The biggest challenge is maintaining the line, being clear about where the people I serve end and where I begin. Also, it is a very lonely place to be, this position of leadership. I cannot be friends with parishioners even though most of them may consider me theirs. Can I sit on someone's deck and have a pint? Sure. I'll listen, ask questions, and get to know them better. However, I'm not going to talk about my personal life or place myself in an overly vulnerable position. I take the advice of a Brian Andreas quote from Story People, "Rules for a successful holiday: 1. Get together with the family 2. Relive old times 3. Get out before it blows."

Finally, I'll get to the real heart of why empathetic preaching is a bad idea: the family is already feeling enough on their own.

It is a great disservice to be so emotive and overly concerned when a family is looking to you for support. If you are a bundle of emotions then you're not doing your job. You are allowing empathy to have the run of the church, and you are likely overfunctioning within the context of the system you have been called to serve.

Israel Galindo, Perspectives on Congregational Leadership: Applying Systems Thinking for Effective Leadership, clarified this concept even further.

"The fact is that, despite the warm metaphor we commonly use, a congregation is not a family. A congregation is a localized, institutionalized expression of a larger social system: the organized religious system. The relationship clergy have with their congregations often leads to seductive enmeshment – even clergy desire their congregations to be family for them, or at the very least "a real community." But until you understand what a congregation is, it's unlikely you'll be able to provide the leadership it needs.

While it's helpful to understand that a congregation is not a family, it often is more helpful to remember that your congregation is not your family. Staying committed to doing one's "family of origin work" will often provide a corrective to this confusion. How often has a pastor not been able to challenge a lay leader who is acting out because that person stirs up emotional process issues related to the father-son or father-daughter relationship in the pastor's family? Or how often has a pastor not been able to provide effective pastoral care for a family in crisis because they find themselves thrust into family emotional processes that strike too close to home? And how many times does a young minister feel crushed and rejected at not being able to be "accepted" by a family size/style church whose members are clearer about family boundaries than the pastor? Unless you are a patriarch pastor of a family church, it's helpful to remember that your congregation is not your family." (59).

There is an obligation we have as leaders of a community; we are to be consistent about how we interact with everyone in the community. Roberta Gilbert talks about this concept extensively in her book *The Cornerstone Concept*.

"The high level leader is a relationship master. He or she connects with people openly, equally and with separate self boundaries. The guideline of openness means connecting; it means staying in open communication with important others – those whom it is important to stay connected with, not only those who are important in group status.

If someone in the group is particularly anxious, one needs to go towards him or her more frequently with an open attitude. Often, these meetings don't need to take much time. They simply need to occur. The very people we shy away from are the ones we need most to make contact with. We will learn the most about managing ourselves in relationships from them – one doesn't learn much from the easy relationships. By the leader making calm connections with the most anxious ones in the group, the organization is spared a great deal of escalating anxiety from within itself.

Equal relationships mean that we don't over- or under-function in relationships." (33).

To go on a bit of a tangent, there is another category of pastor that drives me nuts. It's the pastor who is entitled. Strangely, I know one who oozes empathy to such an extreme that other people's grief becomes his and his alone. I once heard him describe in great detail the lips of a young man who had so much chemotherapy that he swelled up like a big balloon. (This story was repeated to anyone who would listen, primarily: other parishioners). Another time, an ancient man with multiple health issues had died and his developmentally delayed daughter was clearly distraught prior to entering the funeral service for her dad. This same pastor told the family the 'real reason we have sponsors for baptism, because in the early church parents' heads would often be lopped off and someone had to raise the child in the faith.' Seriously?

Again, back to Gilbert:
"The leader who, though in a responsible position, can relate to everyone as his or her equal, is greatly appreciated by everyone. It is a rare person, and it takes skill and practice to develop this ability. Most of us, out of our patterns in our family growing up, tend to feel a little over or a little under others, in relationships. So when we find someone who will relate as an equal, not having all the answers, telling us what to do, or always asking for help – just being there shoulder to shoulder – we know we are in the presence of someone special." (33).

Which brings me to the catalyst for this particular chapter, namely a sermon preached regarding a man who died of a brain tumor. In the setting of the parish I serve, we took on primary and secondary relationships with people who were homebound or going through serious illnesses. In this case my colleague was primary. He did an amazing job with pastoral care, spent hours with the family, and helped the family pray at the onset of the death. It seemed to be what the family needed that informed his pastoral care. The boundaries felt blurred to me but the time he spent was by his choice.

As a result the homily he preached on the day of the funeral made me want to tackle him flat. It was a circular sermon surrounding the Light of Christ and being in Christ's glory: now, face to face. That is not a bad point; in fact, it reminds us not only of death to new life – it brings hope for a day when we will be reunited with those who have gone before us. Unfortunately, that was the only point; light.

We are charged with sharing the good news, not charged with getting so empathetic with those we are tending to that we lose the focus of the gospel. In our dark moments there is Light. The Light is Jesus and takes shape in the community of believers and in the random acts of kindness we receive during difficult times. Jesus will journey with us on this side of the grave because He is all too familiar with that deep, dark hole we call 'death.'

Eventually, we will come to recognize that the Light Shines in the Darkness and the darkness cannot overcome it. But until then, we wait. We sit 'shiva'. We pray. We heal. We rail. We lament. We breathe through the pain because it is the only thing that we can rightly do in our sorrow.

Tom Long wrote in the Introduction to his book, *Accompany Them With Singing,*

> "Yes, funerals provide consolation to those who mourn, but they do so as a part of much broader work involving the retelling of the gospel story, the restoration of meaning, the reaffirmation of the baptismal identity of the one who has died, and the worship of God." (xiv).

He goes on to say,
"Christian pastors have desired to make funerals more personal, more expressive of the desires and lifestyles of the deceased and mourning families, but have ended up allowing them to become more individualistic and even narcissistic. Pastors have tried to make funerals more pastorally sensitive, more comforting to the grief-stricken, but have allowed them to become controlled by psychological rather than theological categories and, therefore, shallower in meaning. Pastors have wanted to free funerals from the morbidity of funeral home cosmetics, but have allowed them to become spiritualized and disembodied. Pastors have desired to make funerals more faithful expressions of hope in the resurrection, but have allowed that strong hope to be edged out by sentimental views of spirituality and immorality." (xv).

Herein lies another example of a member who died at the age of 89. She was a life-long Lutheran and practiced the faith even when she had moved away from the church and into an intentional senior living situation. The stories she told me about the chaplain at the complex were delightful, funny, and engaging. One day, right around Halloween, the chaplain held a service for All Saints Day. She showed up in her costume from the prior night's party; Halloween is the day before All Saints Day. When asked why she did this she simply said, "God knows who I am even if you don't."

As we prepared for her "Witness to the Resurrection" service the oldest daughter wanted nothing to do with the traditional liturgy. She wanted us to use the same service that was used when her son died of a drug overdose sometime during his late thirties. I said, "Well, your mom was Lutheran and you're having the service at her church so it is not going to be modeled after your son's service. It can have elements of that "Celebration of Life" service but it is not going to be exactly the same."
I send out what we do, using the Evangelical Lutheran Worship hymnal. She sent back what she wanted us to do: no psalm, no scripture, no liturgy, no congregational hymns. What's left? A, and I quote, 'A Homily.'

It felt like I was negotiating a deal where I was going to get raked over the coals. There is a time to stand up for the principles of the office and a time to consider the needs of the family. While 'celebrating someone's life' is part of what we are doing when we memorialize someone, we are also participating in the 'work of the people', namely: liturgy. Call and response. It's not a downer; liturgy serves as a ritual that can be a balm of Gilead.

The comparison issue is another aspect of this entire case. More than ever are people basing what they want you to do in a funeral with the actual funerals they have witnessed or participated in. In a quick aside, a widow laid out over a dozen bulletins from funerals she had attended over the last several years and highlighted what she liked and did not like from each one. Then she asked me to make her dearly departed husbands out of the bits she liked.

Funerals are not a smorgasbord for people to dictate to the Church. Rather, funerals are opportunities to say goodbye, hear the good news, and join together in community. We do need to meet people where they are at, for sure! Yet I believe we can still witness the resurrection without the strict use of liturgy. (Since I wrote this in 2015, I have changed my mind on 'imposing' liturgy from a book. Now, I write a liturgy that meets the family where they are at instead of where I'd like them to be.)

Back to the 89 year old whose family wanted an evangelical approach to the service. One of the funnier requests was a time, in the bulletin, for an "Open Mic." I had removed that language and suggested the title, "A Time for Remembrances" reminding the eldest daughter that the service was not a comedy club. That did not go over very well but she did understand why we shifted the language to represent a more eloquent descriptor. (Again, in 2021 retrospect, I would have ABSOLUTELY used the language 'Open Mic' in the bulletin. That's not only light hearted, it summed up the family. As a pastor I am constantly learning and asking for forgiveness when I fail to hear the needs of those I am serving.)
Following the service, the children were grateful for the worship service we provided, maybe not 'over the moon' but grateful. I'll be the first in line to get a pat on the back for a decent sermon or a worship service that was particularly engaging. Most of us need

positive feedback, when it comes to funerals it is my job to stand outside the circle of grief and shine light towards the middle. My grief can come later.

During my first call I officiated a funeral, followed the hearse to the cemetery, talked to the funeral dudes about what sort of Christmas lights they thought were the best, prayed over the coffin "ashes to ashes, dust to dust" and promptly fell apart after the sharing of the peace. I loved the dearly departed. He was a great guy who had a great sense of humor. I did not cry with the family, I cried alone. I cried later that night with my beloved. I allowed the pain of loss to wring me out in the grip of grace. Then, I went back to work and redrew a healthy boundary between myself and the people I had been called to parent.

As for empathy, I'll still go into the ring and battle it out with my social worker friends as a 'very bad idea for pastoral care.' I may not 'win' – but last I checked, life is not about winning or losing – it's about the ride.

In the words of Mark Frost, "Life is not a journey to the grave with the intention of arriving safely in a pretty and well-preserved body. But rather, to skid in broadside, thoroughly used up, totally worn out, and loudly proclaiming .... WOW what a ride." I'm up for a ride, how about you?

Chapter 13: A Grief Absorbed, Sort Of

Grief Absorbed – Sort Of 6.3.19 It's been two and a half years since a predator used pictures of teenage girls faces and superimposed them on some seriously nasty pornography, was arrested, and sentenced to 12.5 years in Federal Prison. This was my associate pastor of seven years.

I have forgiven myself, mostly, over this horrific nodal event in the life of the congregation that I have served for over 16 years now. People tritely say, "Time heals all wounds." To a certain extent that is true but only if you do the harder work. Grief needs words. Grief needs expression.

Grief needs to be absorbed.
"Grief by Gwen Flowers
I had my own notion of grief.
I thought it was the sad time
That followed the death of someone you love.
And you had to push through it
To get to the other side.
But I'm learning there is no other side.
There is no pushing through.
But rather,
There is absorption.
Adjustment.
Acceptance.
And grief is not something you complete,
But rather, you endure.
Grief is not a task to finish

And move on,
But an element of yourself
An alteration of your being.
A new way of seeing.
A new definition of self."

I have learned to redefine myself; not as the former colleague of a very bad, bad man, rather, as someone who has learned a ton about themselves, how systems work, and what one needs to do to not just 'survive' a heinous grievance but 'thrive' despite the crime.
I phrase all of this within the context of predator and crime because that is what happened. Some still want me to openly forgive this person. For me, forgiveness is beyond what I can offer. Also, forgiveness is not for the offender, forgiveness is for the person who endured the trauma, namely: me.

I have finally forgiven myself and for the first time in a very long time: I feel good. I feel like I am nearly whole again. It took a lot of writing. It took friends and colleagues that listened and didn't minimize what I was feeling. It took therapy to unpack betrayal. I had meals with friends. It took a while to learn how to laugh again. It took time and energy and two interims to reset the mission and ministry of the church I serve. It took a tribe of people called ASLC to hold me up when I experienced PTSD following a lawsuit from one of the victims. It took me opening up to my wife, my best friends, and, to the congregational council. It took a ton of work.
I was out to lunch with one of my colleagues who looked at me, just two weeks ago, and said, "Jules, I don't know how you did it, but you were able to look evil in the face and endure it. You did an

amazing job." Just last week, another colleague said, "Jules, we'd go out for lunch about once a quarter, and every time we met you'd be absolutely flummoxed about your former colleague. You stayed the course. You did what you could have done in those moments. You did well. Great, in fact."

A case study was presented at a Clergy System's Seminar that I was facilitating. I listened. I waited. I wondered. Then, I spoke. It seems that those who are addicted to < insert addiction here > can drive just about any leader over the edge. At one point the person presenting said, "By the time this thing is over, I may well be an alcoholic." That is what working with an addict can do to all of our functioning. It's maddening. It's confusing. It's shameful. I felt like I had no worth, when, in fact, that is likely what the predator may have been feeling all along. Worthless.

This does not make me anymore sympathetic to his choices of abuse. In fact, as my current colleague said, just last week, "It wasn't you who encouraged him to click the link that took him to the darkness of child pornography. He made the choice. We all are accountable for our decisions. He decided to go to the link(s) and engage in this horrible behavior. No one can control his decision, his choice."

Another weight dropped. Another absorption of grief. Another moment where someone else understood what I have been through without using platitudes and bullshit. Trauma is real. PTSD is real. It took me a long time to realize that the pain would not go away unless I fully entered into it. And by that, I mean: all in.

Trauma is now in my bones. That's how far the absorption goes. It's not like a cream that one rubs in after a sunburn. This pain goes to the depth of the person we are becoming. It is the hardest work I have ever done – and I did not go it alone. Had I tried, I would have failed.

The most important part of my healing is a group called the After-Care Pastor's Group. I call them the Bat Cave primarily because all of us in the group have experienced different levels of trauma and we talk to each other about our woundedness. They found me. And, in finding me, I started to find myself. We cannot work through this level of trauma alone. We need other people who understand – and – who do not try to 'one-up-another' through their story.

As my friend and colleague Peter says, "It's not the years; it's the mileage." That is truer than I ever imagined. I've sat with that idea for two years now and I believe it.

There is a horrifying inventory called ACES. It is an inventory that assesses childhood trauma. On that inventory I scored a 1. If a child scores 4 or more, life is incredibly difficult to say the least. Here's one of the inventories: https://americanspcc.org/take-the-aces-quiz/

So, in a moment of trying to figure my own trauma out, I created an ACES inventory for pastors.

Adverse Pastorhood Experiences
One point for every number you've experienced any of the following events:

- The funeral of a volunteer youth worker who completed suicide.
- The murder of a former parishioner at age 22. (See Craig's list murder, Shakopee).
- The funeral for a 12-year-old girl who completed suicide.
- The funeral for a baby.
- The funeral of a family killed by a logging truck (grandma+2 grandchildren).
- The funeral of a 29-year-old, newlywed, the week before his stateside reception.
- The funeral of a middle aged woman due to an opioid overdose.
- The funeral of a middle aged woman killed by a distracted driver on the back of a motorcycle.
- The funeral for a 14-year-old boy who completed suicide because of cyberbullying.
- The funeral of a 23-year-old who died from cancer.
- The betrayal of a pastor who embezzled money in order to support his cocaine addiction.
- The arrest of a pastor who sold crack in the basement of the church.
- The church you serve has had one or more clergy sexual misconduct cases.
- The church you serve has had a staff or pastor arrested for on-site pornography use.
- The church you serve has had a pastor arrested for possession and distribution of child pornography and is serving 12.5 years in federal prison (or less/more time).
- The church you serve has kicked off a capital campaign the week following the arrest of the associate pastor.
- You have been called a bitch, dyke, bull-dyke, or a demeaning, hurtful word at some point in your ministry.

- You are in a call where the former pastor manipulated the books to fund pet projects.
- You found your janitor in the basement of the church on Thanksgiving Day, death by suicide.
- Someone exposed themselves to one of your staff.
- You know how to file not just one restraining order but two or more.
- The funeral for a woman murdered by her partner of nearly 30 years, who left 2 sons and 5 grandchildren without parents / grandparents in one act of jealousy.
- You, and / or the church you serve, are being sued. (Add one for each lawsuit).
- The funeral for a 20-year-old who killed his 19-year-old friend and then himself.

If you have 12 or more, it's likely you need an After-Care Pastor group, a good therapist, and a group of people that love you for you outside of your call. That's where I'll leave it tonight.

Chapter 14: A Few Griefs Examined and Examen-ed

Open Your Eyes and Mind Easter 3B, 2024 - a continuation of healing confabulations in the church. Gospel: Luke 24:36b-48

In this account of an appearance after his resurrection, Jesus opens the minds of the disciples to understand him as Messiah. Jesus convinces them that he has been raised and sends them on a mission to proclaim the message of repentance and forgiveness.

36b Jesus himself stood among [the disciples] and said to them, "Peace be with you." 37They were startled and terrified, and thought that they were seeing a ghost. 38He said to them, "Why are you frightened, and why do doubts arise in your hearts? 39Look at my hands and my feet; see that it is I myself. Touch me and see; for a ghost does not have flesh and bones as you see that I have." 40And when he had said this, he showed them his hands and his feet. 41While in their joy they were disbelieving and still wondering, he said to them, "Have you anything here to eat?" 42They gave him a piece of broiled fish, 43and he took it and ate in their presence.

44Then he said to them, "These are my words that I spoke to you while I was still with you—that everything written about me in the law of Moses, the prophets, and the psalms must be fulfilled." 45Then he opened their minds to understand the scriptures, 46and he said to them, "Thus it is written, that the Messiah is to suffer and to rise from the dead on the third day, 47and that repentance and forgiveness of sins is to be proclaimed in his name to all nations, beginning from Jerusalem. 48You are witnesses of these things."

This is the Gospel of Jesus Christ! Thanks be to God.

Sermon: Open Your Eyes and Mind

Recently I was listening to a podcast around the same topic that Pastor Wes preached about last Sunday, namely, why are the Jews so hated?

The answer came swiftly from the commentator: because we need someone to blame, always.

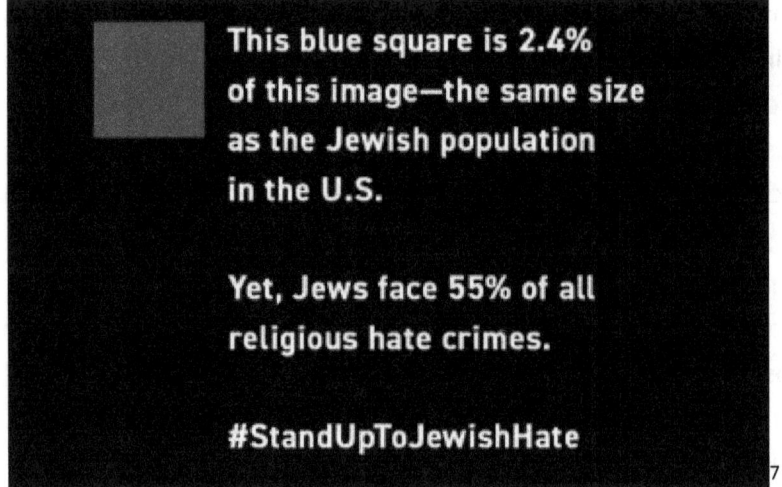

Ouch. The picture above illustrates Jewish people in the blue to the rest of the USA.

We do not like to take personal responsibility for our own words or actions, at least not all the time. Hate travels faster than anything in the entire world.

Words carry power. We hear and see protestors, as well as supporters, to and for different causes.

---

[7] https://jewishheartnj.org/news/jewish-federation-joins-the-foundation-to-combat-antisemitism

We saw people protecting synagogues and mosques after terroristic threats.

We were encouraged, again last week, to consider our Jewish siblings as SIBLINGS - you can have an opinion about the State of Israel and the plight of the Palestinians in Gaza.

I believe we need to Open our Eyes and Minds to become even more like Christ as we care and talk about our neighbors, regardless of race or anything else that is 'different'.

That is the gospel: Love one Another; Love God with everything you've got.

As Martin Luther got GRACE right, he also failed the Jewish people by some of his lesser writings.

So today I wanted to take just a few minutes sharing with you about another theologian that helped shape many of my own understanding surrounding the Christian faith.
Dietrich Bonhoeffer was just as complicated as Luther in many ways.

The book that I am most familiar with is titled *Life Together* and that is exactly what the book discusses.
Here's one quote to give you a taste of what he believed:
"The person who loves their dream of community will destroy community, but the person who loves those around them will create community."

And again: "The first service one owes to others in a community involves listening to them.

Just as our love for God begins with listening to God's Word, the beginning of love for others is learning to listen to them.
God's love for us is shown by the fact that God not only gives God's Word, but also lends us God's ear."

"We do God's work for our brothers and sisters when we learn to listen to them.

So often Christians, especially preachers, think that their only service is always to have to 'offer' something when they are together with other people.

They forget that listening can be a greater service...Christians who can no longer listen to one another will soon no longer be listening to God either."

I mention these two quotes because Bonhoeffer was a force to be reckoned with when faced with Hitler.

Eric Metaxas wrote a biography that is a door stop size: 624 pages. Are you ready to stay for a while?

Here's a summary of Bonhoeffer: Pastor, Martyr, Prophet, Spy.
"Who better to face the greatest evil of the 20th-century than a humble man of faith?

As Adolf Hitler and the Nazis seduced a nation, bullied a continent, and attempted to exterminate the Jews of Europe, a small number of dissidents and saboteurs worked to dismantle the Third Reich from the inside.

Metaxas presents the fullest accounting of Bonhoeffer's heart-wrenching decision to leave the safe haven of America to return to Hitler's Germany, and sheds new light on Bonhoeffer's involvement in the famous Valkyrie plot and in "Operation 7," the effort to smuggle Jews into neutral Switzerland.

In a deeply moving narrative, Metaxas uses previously unavailable documents including personal letters, detailed journal entries, and firsthand personal accounts to reveal dimensions of Bonhoeffer's life and theology never before seen."

Bonhoeffer, a former pacifist, was also a participant in the German Resistance movement against Nazism, a founding member of the Confessing Church.

His involvement in plans by members of the Abwehr (the German Military Intelligence Office) to assassinate Adolf Hitler resulted in his arrest in April 1943 and his subsequent execution by hanging in April 1945, shortly before the war's end.

While incarcerated he wrote: *Letters And Papers From Prison*, here are a few more quotes:

- "We must learn to regard people less in the light of what they do or omit to do, and more in the light of what they suffer."

- "Jesus himself did not try to convert the two thieves on the cross; he waited until one of them turned to him."
- "In normal life we hardly realize how much more we receive than we give, and life cannot be rich without such gratitude. It is so easy to overestimate the importance of our own achievements compared with what we owe to the help of others."

We don't go it alone, we were never meant to.

As Jesus appeared to the disciples after the resurrection, he opened their eyes and their minds to understand all that he had done and said.

Jesus took the fish and ate it. Remember, he took the fish and bread and blessed it and all 5,000 men, not counting women and children, ate their fill.

On the road to Emmaus, the disciples' eyes were also opened at the breaking of the bread. They said to one another: Did our hearts not burn within us when Jesus opened to us the Scriptures?

Can our eyes and our minds be opened to understanding the power of the resurrection in the same way?

Word of life, Jesus Christ, all glory to you! Word of life, Jesus Christ, all praise to you!
Our hearts burn within us while you open to us the Scriptures. Word of life, Jesus Christ, all glory to you! Word of life, Jesus Christ, all praise to you!

I want your eyes and your minds and your hearts to be open to the possibility that we don't always get it right, too.

Bonhoeffer didn't get everything right.

He wrote things that were harmful, things that were not helpful to people of faith, namely the book, *The Cost of Discipleship*. Bonhoeffer said he wished he never wrote it.

I mention this last bit because we can learn and grow from our mistakes without taking everyone else out at the kneecaps. Bonhoeffer, by the way, was the reason Beth became a theologian and someone who loves God wholeheartedly.

He helped her delineate between what the church 'told her' to be (the should, ought, have to) specifically how 'the church' told her what she would have to do in order to get to heaven.

Whereas, Bonhoeffer taught her to ask the questions: Who do you want to be? How do you want to be in this world at this time? What are the choices you are going to make?

It's about being present in this world and being accountable for your behavior now. It's about being in right relationship with God and with the neighbor that drives you a bit wonky.

Ultimately, what I took away from this conversation with Beth about her favorite theologian was this:

What kind of legacy do you want to leave behind?

One that is generous with your love, service, heart, and gratitude? Or, the opposite?

Who do you get to be in this world? A beloved child of God.

Because Jesus tells the disciples and us, over and over and over again: I AM here with you.

And for this good news we can all say: Thanks be to God. Amen.

A Grief Re-Examined, Part 2
19 October 2017

Grief is grief. It'll take as long as it will take. I know there is no timeline. There is no end. Here's my struggle: what if the grief is so much deeper than those around you that you're not sure what to do. Kara said to me last night, "That has got to be the last article that you mention 'the event', we are done with it, done with Bill." Then, shortly thereafter she was cleaning out the copy room, came across 5 packages of 4"x6" photo paper and asked, "What is this doing in here?" I said, "It came from the other person's office." She picked it up and slammed it in the trash. Rage. Good, justified rage. I left the space. I feel like that short interchange gave her an idea of the constant work we've done over the last year to eradicate his presence from the place.

It is four days short of the most nodal event I have experienced in my professional career. I know I handled it well. I was aplomb, courageous, and I have been rising strong ever since. Yet, I have days when I am wobbly, weary, and still overwhelmed by the sheer sadness and terror that was inflicted upon our community. These last two weeks, as I have made my way toward this anniversary date of the nodal event, I have been pummeling my body through fitness to let go of the pain. I have eaten less, lost some weight, had nightmares, and, in general, felt really down. I know I am not depressed – probably because I have done the hard work on behalf of my body. I am trying really hard to get over this and move on. I am trying very hard not to talk about 'all the time' even though I know I am not doing that – it's just an internal wheel in my mind that keeps on spinning.

When I write, I think about God. I wonder how this man I trusted could actually dehumanize not only the cropped photos of people I loved, confirmed, taught, and mentored, but also those of the images they were superimposed upon? Then I ask myself, am I dehumanizing him? Does that make sense? I think people who are predatory need to be locked up, placed outside of the circle. That is a good boundary. I am wondering if what I need to do is get to a place where I can forgive him…not in the sense that 'all is forgiven' or 'all forgotten'. Neither would be true. But I am carrying a pretty big hurt here and I wonder what would happen if I said the words out loud? People have told me that "I need to forgive him" or "I should forgive him" and "done is done, he is not our problem anymore, he is getting what he deserves." I am not in the camp of "should" "ought" or "have to's" so that sort of recommendation does not work for me; it feels like shame because it is shame. We have got to STOP doing that to each other. We have got to create a place, a space where people can go at their own pace when it comes to grief, forgiveness, or anything else for that matter.

The last time I checked, forgiveness is not for the offender. It is for me. I forgave myself for not being able to protect our community, our Ubuntu. No one could have protected us, even though I do believe I have some super powers, namely, teaching people how to forgive themselves and move into a brighter future. I do this primarily by serving and loving others well. Then I do it all over again. And, again. Until I feel better about not feeling very good about this grief process.

If I forgave him for being an addict, for hurting our children, would it allow a part of me loose, a part of me to be free? Perhaps. I'm not sure I am emotionally ready to lean that far. I'm pretty used to living in the arena and kicking my own ass. Only three people know first-hand how difficult this has been for me. They see me fully. Love me for free. Marvel at my fortitude and calm. I marvel, too. How did I make it through this with such grace and poise, aplomb? Maybe it really was God working through me despite me.

I know I need to move on. Let go. Forgive. As Anne Lamott said, "Not forgiving is like drinking rat poison and waiting for the rat to die." I don't feel like I am dying, just crying. I don't feel poisoned, just deeply wounded. I don't feel like I am going to break, I feel stronger and clearer about who I am and who I am becoming than I ever have before. The fullness of being 'Just Jules' has been an amazing gift throughout this entire process.

There have been some excellent conversations about moving on, with both Jim the Elder and James the Younger. Both kind men will help us move into a better future with the gospel at the center, love in action, and a sense of ownership for the community I serve. I said at Bible study today, "You all need to claim this church as your own. I am here to serve you but this is not my church. Be a part of the visioning. Be a part of the process. I want to leave this place in better shape than I found it. That is the campsite rule that I adhere to." It gave this tight-knit small group some food for thought: PJ may leave. I may, but there is some work to be done first. Why are you here? What are you called to do? How will you live out the mission and ministry of Jesus Christ should I not be in the mix? What does that look like?

What I know as my own truth is that I love what I do. I'm good at what I do. I have a passion for preaching and teaching, marrying and burying, baptizing and confirming. Daily I am amazed but not surprised at the acts of kindness I see through the volunteerism and connectivity of this community. I am affirmed for my gifts. People are ever so grateful for worship services that are full of grace and energy, gratitude and vision, music and words that create a space of wonderment and transformation.

I would bear this grief all over again. I have learned so much about myself, this tribe, and what it means to live the BRAVING practice. I know I will have other griefs to bear, that is the nature of being human. In the meantime, I will ponder forgiveness. I just might be the part that needs to happen in order for me to move on, move through the grief I have carried over the last year.

That's where I will leave it tonight.

Chapter 15: A Sermon for Parent(s) who are grieving
If You Fall
11.10.19
All Saints Lutheran Church, ELCA
The Rev. Dr. Jules Erickson

Artist: JJ Heller
Song: If You Fall (Acoustic)
https://www.youtube.com/watch?v=ztBPBsbkvFQ
Pastor Tanner Howard and I sang this together at the beginning of the sermon.

As many of you know, my niece and nephew had twin daughters that died within a day of their birth. At just barely over a pound, Sage left us first. 12 hours later, Sloane followed her sister into the light of Christ.

We got the call on Tuesday morning that Sloane had died and we were totally devastated.

Beth is not only Amanda's Aunt, she is her godmother. She said to me: I have no words.

I didn't either.

We got ready and got in the car. That's when she let someone else talk for her.

She turned on Spotify, that's where we keep all of our music, and started playing IF YOU FALL by JJ Heller – over and over and over again.

As we made our way to North Memorial, we took the long way, 62 to France, up to Excelsior Blvd., all along Cedar Lake Parkway – to the sparkling lakes that wind in between Theodore Wirth Parkway.

It felt like a funeral procession, because it was.

The songs she played you may be familiar with, as I have shared some of them with all of you over the years: Gabriel's Oboe, Hymn to Hope, Deep Peace, 'Tis a Gift to be Simple, and Blessings by Laura Story.

"Blessings" is printed in your bulletin for you to consider over this next week.

We pray for blessings
We pray for peace Comfort for family, protection while we sleep We pray for healing, for prosperity We pray for Your mighty hand to ease our suffering All the while, You hear each spoken need Yet love is way too much to give us lesser things
'Cause what if your blessings come through raindrops What if Your healing comes through tears What if a thousand sleepless nights are what it takes to know You're near What if trials of this life are Your mercies in disguise

A twelfth-century poem reads:

'Tis a fearful thing
To love
What death can touch
To love, to hope, to dream,
And oh, to lose.
A thing for fools, this,
Love,
But a holy thing
To love what death can touch.

This is but one thing we all have in common.
Sorrow. Loss. Grief. Sadness.

I wonder if that is why we, along with the Sadducees, wonder what heaven might look like?

I see a sign beside the road on highway 61 that reads:
HEAVEN IS COMING: Are You Ready?

And I think to myself: Is anyone?

Life, this life, is not about trying to get to heaven – it's not about what we do or do not do.

The resurrection life has already been given to all of us.

Our preoccupation about the afterlife would be smart to give up.

Why? Because of the answer that Jesus gave, to those who could hear, in our gospel text for today.

It was a common practice 2,000 years ago for a man to take the widow of his brother following the brother's death to protect her from poverty and homelessness.

The question: If seven brothers married the same woman – which– then when you get to heaven, how does that actually work?

Jesus' response: you are all God's children, children of the resurrection.

God is not the God of the dead, but of the living, for to God, we are all alive.

Yet, what we all have in common is: Sorrow. Loss. Grief. Sadness.

Now here Jesus is saying that there is no difference to God between the living and the dead.   We are all one in Christ Jesus.   We are all children of God.
What we are called to do is the hard work of grief when it comes around.

Naomi Nye wrote:
"Before you know kindness as the deepest thing inside,
You must know sorrow as the other deepest thing.
You must wake up with sorrow.
You must speak it till your voice
Catches the thread of all sorrows

And you see the size of the cloth."

What grief dares us to do is to love again – again and again and again.

We are called to trust in the resurrection life, in the here and now, in the time that is to come.

Let's help each other in this journey, this arduous task of taking care of one another in the dark places of our lives.

The last song that Beth played as we completed our funeral procession was the song we will now sing as a congregation: Will You Let Me Be Your Servant?

This is our call as children of God.

And for this good news, we can all say: Thanks be to God. Amen.

Prayers of Intercession
United with the saints of every time and place, let us pray for the church, those in need, and all of God's creation, responding with the song: hear my prayer, hear my prayer, Lord make me whole.

Loving Redeemer, by grace you have chosen us to live boldly as resurrection people. Strengthen us to stand firm and proclaim the good news to the world.
Maker of all, you bless us with the change of seasons. Create safe pathways as plants and animals prepare for winter, and make us good stewards of your bountiful creation. Hear us as we sing:

Divine judge, your justice and mercy are revealed to us in your steadfast love. Grant rest and peace to our faithful veterans, and give courage to government officials who lead, serve, and protect. Listening God, your beloved people call to you and you answer them. Hear the cries of those who are poor and unemployed, those who seek refuge, those who suffer from addiction, and all who are sick (especially). Guard and keep them in your loving care. Hear us as we sing.

Generous teacher, you look upon your children with a loving heart. Bless the ministries of those who work with, serve, teach, and lead children.

God of the living, to you all are alive. We give thanks for those who have died in the faith especially Sage and Sloane and all that we name in this time and space. Give us joy in knowing that our Redeemer lives, and that we will be united with the faithful in a resurrection like his. Hear us as we sing!

Rejoicing in hope, we lift our prayers to you, most gracious Lord, trusting that you have received them in your care. Amen.

Part Two

Holding On
All Saints Sunday 2020
All Saints Lutheran, ELCA
The Rev. Dr. Jules Erickson

Grace and peace to you, beloved people of God!

One year ago, this coming weekend, will mark the anniversary of our niece and nephew's twin daughters birthday and death day and baptismal birthday.

I wrote a sermon titled, "If You Fall," a title after a J.J. Heller song, which Pastor Tanner and I sung within the sermon itself.

Please, if you have not heard it, go to our podcast through the sermon tab on our website and scroll down to If You Fall (11/10).

Sloane Eliza and Sage Adair were sooooo loved. They still are; they will always hold a precious place in our hearts, in our entire family's hearts.

We played one of my favorite playlists that I had created on Spotify, one I had named "Holding On."

It seems that we've all been Holding On of late.

Holding on to sanity.

Holding on to one another.

Holding on to the hope that one day we can see, touch, and hold one another's hands again as we pray the prayer Jesus taught us.

We have been navigating significant change in our world, in our country, in our cities, and in our homes.

Thank goodness we have the ability to stay connected through telephone calls, computer screens, and socially distanced walk-talks.

And, as we have said from the very beginning of this Covid-19 pandemic, though we are a distributed community, we are not alone, ESPECIALLY in our grief.

We have had to change the way we do things, for sure, but we do go through life alone.

Sharon Salzberg, a Buddhist teacher and renowned author came out with her latest book last week. Its title is *Real Change: Mindfulness to Heal Ourselves and the World.*

I'd like to share a portion with you this morning as we navigate grief and loss, and the joy that comes in the morning.

Salzberg wrote:

"We don't live in isolated silos, disconnected from everybody else — it just feels that way sometimes. What happens to others inevitably affects us.

Even if we have been ignoring or unaware of the situation of those we don't know, we can wake up and see that our lives are actually intricately connected.

What happens 'over there' never nicely stays 'over there' — it flows out. And what we do over here matters.

This interconnectedness is not only a spiritual realization —
science shows us this, economics shows us this,
environmental awareness certainly shows us this,
and even epidemiology shows us this."

In other words, we are all holding on to one another, even when it does not feel that way.

Can you begin to imagine hearing the words that Jesus shared to those who were longing for hope on a hillside?

People who are just nearly holding on?
The crowds have found him and are yearning for a word of hope.
Let's set the scene, Jesus' ministry of holding on to those began quickly.

Back in Ch. 4 Jesus had been put to the test by Satan, began preaching, called the disciples, healed the sick, those suffering from pain, the demon-possessed, those afflicted with seizures, the paralyzed.

One by one, not 'silo-ed', he prayed and blessed, and then blessed some more.

Connecting them and us to an incredible reminder that while we are all Holding On, we are not alone.

AND: What we do over here matters, as Salzberg wrote.

We are and will continue to be 'blessed.

We are blessed when:
our spirits are depleted,
when we are mourning.
For whenever we are feeling wobbly, we are reminded that:
We are God's beloved children.
We will be comforted.
We have been given all that we need.

We are blessed when:
We have the opportunity to be merciful.
When we allow God to create a clean heart and renew a right spirit within us.
For when we create space where Peace is present,
we WILL be called children of God.

We are God's children, we are held, we are loved for free, we are blessed, over and over and over again.

This next weekend, on the anniversary of our twin baby girls, Sloane and Sage's birthday and death day and baptismal birthday, we will pray our goodbyes.

Gathering at the family home in Esko, we will bless, bless, bless. Because: What we do over here matters.

And, what I will remind Amanda and Cory, and our extended family, is a summary of what you have just heard, and this:

SOME THINGS CANNOT BE FIXED.
    THEY CAN ONLY BE CARRIED.

Megan Devine wrote that truth.

In her book, *It's OK That You're Not OK: Meeting Grief and Loss in a Culture that Doesn't Understand*, she said:

"The reality of grief is far different from what others see from the outside.
There is pain in this world that you can't be cheered out of.
You don't need solutions.
You don't need to move on from your grief.
You need someone to see your grief, to acknowledge it.
You need someone to HOLD your hands while you stand there in blinking horror, staring at the hole that was your life.

Some things cannot be fixed. They can only be carried."

People, beloved people of God, know that whatever you are carrying today, we are here, as the hands and feet of Jesus, as a community of faith, to help you while you're holding on.

You are blessed, you are beloved, you are the children of God.

And for this good news, we can all say: Thanks be to God. Amen.

—

Author's note:
This in no way 'concludes' my commentary on grief.

I'm not an 'expert' on anything other than doing the very best I can as I wander through this world. You may not 'like' the content. You may argue with some of the words I have written or preached. That's okay, just keep the comments to yourself.

We live in a 'knee-jerk' reactive world.

How about we all give each other a good measure of grace?

Whenever I write, 'That's where I'll leave it tonight', that's what I'll encourage you to do as well. Let go, lean in, feel it all, breathe, repeat.

Thank you for taking the time to read my reflections. I hope they will help you as you navigate your own grief and begin to understand that we all carry heavy burdens.

What I have learned: none of us has to go alone, we were never meant to.

From your still working on sorting things out author,

Jules

The Rev. Dr. Jules Erickson has served as a Minister of Word and Sacrament in the ELCA since she was ordained in 1996. She is a Clergy Coach, an Adjunct Professor at Luther Seminary, leads a Rostered Clergy class on BFST, and loves to preach, teach, play and create pottery. Jules is also a Certified Facilitator for The Daring Way™ and Rising Strong™ Curricula from the research of Brené Brown. She lives in Hastings with her wife and their two golden doodles. If you want to have a guest speaker or need a coach, contact Jules at jules@allsaintscg.org Check out more about the parish she serves at www.allsaintscg.org Stay tuned for upcoming book releases on the topics: Jules' Musings: Stories of Tails & Tales; "Stuff" They Don't Teach You in God School; and a children's book titled The Maple Leaf.

www.ingramcontent.com/pod-product-compliance
Lightning Source LLC
Chambersburg PA
CBHW050906160426
43194CB00011B/2303